Adelaide Tagliabue Hatch

THE NATIVES OF ENGLAND

THE NATIVES

OF

ENGLAND

HENRY WOODD NEVINSON

With sixteen plates by
C. R. W. NEVINSON

19 31

New York: ALFRED·A·KNOPF

"Lords and Commons of England, consider what Nation it is whereof ye are and whereof ye are the governours: a Nation not slow and dull, but of a quick, ingenious, and piercing spirit, acute to invent, suttle and sinewy to discours, not beneath the reach of any point the highest that human capacity can soar to."

John Milton: *Areopagitica* (1644).

PREFACE

WHEN I was out as a war correspondent with the Bulgarian Army in the first Balkan War (1912), I happened to be sitting in a devastated café with a French correspondent — the same, I am told, who won fame three years later by shouting *"Debout les morts!"* — during a ferocious German assault at Verdun. At all events, he was a typical Frenchman and a true patriot, for he spent the evening in pouring characteristic abuse upon the English. To him we as a nation were mean, money-grubbing, hypocritical, ill-mannered, inartistic, and hideous. Being far from home, short of food, and having found loathsome insects in the soup, I was irritated into an unreasoning patriotism in defence of my country, and at last was driven to the fatuous assertion: "At all events, we say what we mean, and mean what we say!" "That is exactly why we hate you!" came the rapid reply.

If other races hate us for what we think our virtues, no wonder it is hard to please them. To myself it seems quite impossible for one race ever to understand another, even though closely connected by origin, as we are with the Germans and Americans. They may talk our language "like natives," but they remain blind and deaf to the inner and hidden meanings buried in almost every word. Take such a common English word as " home." The Germans use " house" where we say "home," and the Americans use "home " where we say "house." Neither race fully understands our word — its associations, its background, its half-realized connection with our length of history and literature. Or take such a word as " mariner." All the races of Europe would translate it by their words for " sailor." But to us " mariner" suggests ever so much more than "sailor." No foreigner could perceive the shade of contempt that has fallen on " philanthropy" or "charity." Or take the common word "lady." To us it is surrounded by a cloud of meanings dimly perceptible to ourselves, but to foreigners as nonexistent as ghosts. Indeed, these inner meanings are family ghosts, and only we can feel their presence.

So we must give up hope of being intimately understood by any other race, just as we on our part can understand no foreigners, no matter how well we may appear to speak their language or try to imitate their habits. Want of understanding generally produces hatred, as in the case of my French war-correspondent, and when we hate a man we hate all he does. We hate his work, and we hate his virtues, if he has any. Often in Dublin, after a delightful evening spent among my Irish friends, who give me such a welcome as I receive nowhere else,

I have come away feeling as though I had been exquisitely operated upon for a disease I never had. That was simply because I was infected by their hatred for the English. In a less degree I have suffered at the hands of Indians, Americans, and Boers; for we English are all exposed to a kind of generic hatred, and the sins of our fathers are visited upon us, even when our fathers have not sinned.

The praise that comes from want of understanding is much rarer, because blind-eyed affection, which produces praise, is much rarer than blind-eyed hatred, and much more difficult to maintain. Indeed, in most of the praise that foreigners have bestowed upon us there is a touch of ironic disparagement that we thoroughly enjoy. Has the great Irish critic ever praised us? I cannot remember, but it is his unremitting disparagement that makes Bernard Shaw the most popular writer. How acceptable has been the irony closely mingled with the commendation in Taine, Anatole France, Madariaga, Karel Čapek, Dibelius, and others whom I have quoted in this little book! We listen with pleasure to all this detraction, or, as Carlyle said, we listen with godlike indifference. Recent historians are fond of pleasing us by quoting that passage from a Venetian Ambassador, who said (1497), "the English are great lovers of themselves and of everything belonging to them. They think there are no other men like themselves and no other world but

England; and whenever they see a handsome foreigner, they say that he looks like an Englishman, and that it is a great pity he should not be an Englishman."[1] That is no doubt still true of a certain type of Englishman. It reminds one of Bishop Creighton's saying, " An Oxford man walks as if the whole world belonged to him. A Cambridge man walks as if he didn't care a damn whom the world belonged to." Here is flattery mixed with the ridicule, and we like the mixture.

Many foreigners are irritated when they find among us something quite different from their expectations. I have known Americans revel, as well they may, in the beauty of the Life Guards, Westminster Abbey, Oxford, Chiddingstone, and similar mossy old things they expected, but lose all enthusiasm for England at the sight of Kentish Town, Peckham, Oldham, Regent Street, or other realities that are not mossy. I know a brilliant foreign critic who extravagantly praises the rollicking, roundabout, beery, hangman English of a century ago — the English he knew from his special period of study — but thinks the greatness of the country began to fade away about 1830, and has now vanished. When an English friend and I were invited by a German professor to share some fungi he had gathered in the woods during the starvation in the Ruhr (1923), and we had no difficulty in recognizing his quotations from our own literature, he said rather sadly,

[1] Quoted, among others, by Dean Inge in *England*, p. 43.

"You give me quite a new conception of English-men!"

But in our hearts we English understand our-selves fairly well, and some of our race, either owing to our natural modesty, or for fear of easy self-satisfaction, or in a spirit of universal indignation, are rather inclined to join the Frenchman in decry-ing even such fine qualities as they may discover among our obvious iniquities. It is their very affec-tion for our peculiar people that makes them thus critical and apprehensive. Their jealousy for the country's honour may even spring from that pas-sion of affectionate understanding expressed in a favourite passage of mine, written probably at least 150 years ago, by Halifax, whom they called the Trimmer:

"Our Trimmer," he said, "is far from Idolatry in other things, in one thing only he cometh near it, his Country is in some degree his Idol; he doth not worship the Sun, be-cause 'tis not peculiar to us, it rambles round the world, and is less kind to us than to others; but for the Earth of England, though perhaps inferior to that of many places abroad, to him there is Divinity in it, and he would rather dye than see a spire of English Grass trampled down by a Foreign Trespasser: He thinketh there are a great many of his mind, for all plants are apt to taste of the Soyl in which they grow, and we that grow here have a root that produceth in us a stalk of English Juice, which is not to be changed by grafting or foreign infusion; and I do not know whether anything less will prevail, than the Modern Experiment, by which the Blood of one Creature is trans-mitted into another; according to which, before the French blood can be let into our bodies, every drop of our own must be drawn out of them."[1]

A good many excellent books have lately been written upon our subject, especially by foreign critics, who write so easily because they know so little; for we are all aware that ignorance makes generalities easy. Among the very best of these foreign writers I should put Professor Dibelius (*England*), Professor Santayana (*Soliloquies in England*), Carl Silex (*John Bull zu Hause*), André Siegfried (*Post-War Britain*, mainly commercial), Professor de Madariaga (*Englishmen, Frenchmen, and Spaniards*), Karel Čapek (*Letters from England*), Rudolf Kircher (*Pillars and Powers* and *Fair Play, the Games of Merrie England*), and (*Wie die Engländer's machen*), André Maurois (*Études Anglaises*), and Bernard Shaw (*passim*, but especially *John Bull's Other Island* and *Heartbreak House*).

Among recent English writers I might mention Dean Inge (*England*), Stanley Baldwin (*Our Inheritance*), Havelock Ellis (*Study of British Genius*), J. B. Priestley (*English Humour*), Bernard Darwin (*The English Public School*), Professor Mawer (*Problems of Place Name Study*), Dr. A. D. Lindsay (*The Essentials of Democracy*), C. F. G. Masterman (*The Condition of England*), Eric Parker (*English Wild Life*), Anthony Collett (*The*

[1] George Savile, First Marquess of Halifax, *The Character of a Trimmer* (published 1700, but written earlier).

Changing Face of England), C. E. Montague (*The Right Place* and *A Writer's Notes on his Trade*), Horace Annesley Vachell (*The Best of England, mainly sport*), Thomas Burke (*The English Inn*), Neville Cardus (*Cricket*), Evelyn Sharp (*The London Child* and *The Child Grows Up*), George Bourne (*The Bettesworth Book*), N. Niemeyer and E. W. Spalding (*Piers Plowman Social and Economic Histories; Book VII,* 1830 *to Present Day*), the famous Economic Historians, Lord Passfield and Mrs. Sidney Webb, and Mr. and Mrs. J. L. Hammond. I may also mention my own sixpenny book, *The English,* of which this volume is an expansion.

I think I have founded most of the book upon my own experience and observation during a long life, chiefly spent among my own countrymen. But I have, of course, absorbed much from the works of such writers as Dickens, Meredith, Hardy, Galsworthy, and Arnold Bennett.

My son's pictures included in the book are not intended as " illustrations," but are small reproductions of pictures painted or drawn by him without any connection with my work.

H. W. N.

London, 1930.

CONTENTS

LIST OF PICTURES

THE NATIVES

OF

ENGLAND

CHAPTER I

THE ISLAND SCENE

"This blessed plot, this earth."
King Richard II, Act II, Scene 1.

WHEN TENNYSON, in his "Ode on the Death of the Duke of Wellington," wrote of "our rough island-story," he was perhaps thinking of the people as being rough rather than of the land. Yet he had in mind our country too, for earlier in the Ode he calls upon the nation to "thank Him who isled us here, and roughly set His Saxon in blown seas and storming showers." And, what is even more conclusive, he later on converts this phrase "rough island-story" into "fair island-story," thus suggesting two opposite qualities conjoined in our country as in our people. Tennyson's knowledge of the English island-scene, especially on its fairer side, was singularly exact and without question he recognized its intimate connection with the inhabitants, whom he habitually regarded also on their fairer side.

The island itself so far as the English inhabit it (up to the Solway, the Cheviots, and the Tweed in the north, and as far as the less distinctive borders of Wales on the west) may similarly be divided into "rough" and "fair," or north and south, the division following the course of the Trent, though not very exactly. Nature has thus divided the islanders themselves into northerners and southerners, and her influence can be traced in the character of both. The distinction is obvious to ourselves, but to foreigners and to history we shall probably remain rough islanders for many generations to come, though the part of the country which we call fair is almost the only part that foreigners visit.

It is no wonder they are attracted by the south, for the south is a country of peculiar beauty. It is a land of low hills and running downs, of quiet but not torpid rivers, spanned by bridges of weathered stone, and lined with tall reeds and yellow iris along the banks of pastures where cattle browse in freedom. The trees are oak, beech, ash, and line upon line of elms planted among hedgerows dividing field from field. Large stretches of former forests and commons remain, and one may still find grassy parks, where ancient oaks grow older. Some of the soil is sandy, fit for pines, and some is moorland, rocky and covered with heather or ling. But most of it is good for plough or pasture — "fit to smear on bread," as an admiring visitor has written.[1] Except upon the few chalk ranges, like the Chilterns, water is everywhere abundant, and, according to season, all the fields and ditches are full of flowers. It is especially a land of gardens. Almost every cot-

---

[1] *Letters from England*, by Karel Čapek, p. 80.

tage in the grey stone villages of such counties as Wilts and Gloucestershire has its brilliant patch of flowers before the door, and many gardens around the old halls and farms are of formal beauty. Thus the southern country still retains the charm of " A Midsummer Night's Dream," and our poets through the line of Milton, Andrew Marvell, Collins, and Tennyson, down to some still living, have sung of it with tender attachment to the very earth. Even Pope, in a mood of aberration, attempted to cast it into couplets.

It is difficult to select a passage from the many poems suggesting the beauty of this part of England; whether to choose from one of the poets mentioned already, or from Matthew Arnold's " Scholar Gypsy " or Browning's " Home-Thoughts from Abroad." Among the best would stand William Blake's " Night," beginning:

> " The sun descending in the west,
> The evening star does shine;
> And birds are silent in their nest,
> And I must seek for mine.
> The moon, like a flower,
> In heaven's high bower,
> With silent delight
> Sits and smiles on the night."

The eastern counties are of different character from the rest of the southern land. Apart from very low hills, wolds, and islands of slight elevation, upon which ancient shrines were sometimes built, as at

Crowland, Peterborough, and Ely, the country was once largely fen. But for one or two small patches, chiefly preserved for their interest to naturalists, the fens have left little evidence of their former liquid condition, except the rich black earth and the dikes from which the water was pumped up to higher levels so as to reach the sea. The large expanses of salt or brackish water lying between the fenland and the sea are, for the most part, separated from the fens by low barriers of land, and at some points along the coast, as at Aldeburgh, the sea itself has cast up a barrier of shingle which diverts the out-flow even of a river. The beauty of the eastern counties lies in the vast dome of the sky, the windmills, the bridges, the sails of barges that seem to be moving over dry land, and the towers of churches and cathedrals conspicuous as ships upon a distant horizon. Crabbe and Cowper are the characteristic poets of these eastern counties. But perhaps for all his romanticism, we should add William Morris, an Essex man. And, after all, the man who wrote the exquisite verse in "Maud" beginning "All night have the roses heard," came from Lincoln-shire.

In Morris, as in Ruskin, and many of our recent poets, we feel a certain wistfulness, a longing to retain a beauty already vanishing from sight and reach. They desire passionately to cling to all that is left of it, and to enjoy it while they may. But their enjoyment is tinged with the sadness of mutability.

Those wooded hills and quiet rivers, meadows, orchards, ploughed fields, mill-streams, garden walls, and grey old villages have been disappearing before their eyes, and they would sanctify their relics. A yearning for England's past has spread among all who are sensitive to beauty, and many who have known nothing of the country except on Saturday afternoons or week-ends are so anxious to catch the precious fragments of it that the village streets of Broadway in Gloucestershire or Burford near Oxford are invisible under their crowding cars and motor-coaches. There is need of haste. Within a century the railways have destroyed much of the ancient beauty so regretfully sought. And no one can foretell what motor-cars, coaches, and arterial roads, fringed with bungalows, may not soon destroy.

Beautiful antiquity is also threatened by tall rows of pylons transmitting electricity from distant power-stations. And still another danger comes from the passion of wealthy Americans for England's ancient furniture, mossy cottages, and picturesque decay. In the hope of possessing their beauty by transplanting it to their own country, they now at great expense remove not only old chairs, china, settles, and chests, but whole buildings, stone by stone to alien sites in the United States. Their admiration is commendable, and we may envy the wealth which can thus take advantage of our national impoverishment. But one might refer these

acquisitive enthusiasts, as well as our own æsthetic
week-enders, to that sonnet of Wordsworth which
says :

" Yes, there is holy pleasure in thine eye!
   — The lovely cottage in the guardian nook
Hath stirred thee deeply; with its own dear brook,
Its own small pasture, almost its own sky!
But covet not the Abode; forbear to sigh,
As many do, repining while they look;
Intruders, who would tear from Nature's book
This precious leaf, with harsh impiety.
Think what the Home must be if it were thine,
Even thine, though few thy wants! — Roof, window, door,
The very flowers are sacred to the Poor;
The roses to the porch which they entwine.
Yea, all, that now enchants thee, from the day
On which it should be touched, would melt away."

Struggling to preserve something of England's
vanishing characteristics and vanishing beauty, various societies have been happily formed, such as
the National Trust, the Commons Preservation Society, the Council for the Preservation of Rural
England, the Committees for Regional Town-
Planning, and local societies for Oxford and Cambridge. A good many beautiful scenes have been
saved for the country by the generosity of private
people, some even by the wisdom of public bodies.
By such means one may hope that something of
England's peculiar charm may be preserved for at
least another hundred years, and after that time the
ideal of beauty may have completely changed as in

the eighteenth century, and the associations of tradition may be obliterated.

In the southern country there are a few hills that might almost be called mountains, such as the isolated Wrekin, Caradoc, and the Long Mynd of Shropshire, the Malvern Hills, and the low range of Charnwood Forest in Leicestershire, now being quarried away for its granite. And there are still wastes that keep the name of forest or chace, such as the New Forest, Epping Forest, the Forest of Dean, Savernake Forest in Wilts, Ashdown Forest in Sussex, Cannock Chace, Cranborne Chace, and a few others. But the north has higher mountains and wider wastes, forests, and moors. The Cheviot Hills, the outlying mountains of Cumberland and Westmorland, and the long backbone of the Pennine range, running from Cumberland down through Derbyshire, have given a wilder and sterner aspect to all the northern country. So have the expanses of moorland in Northumberland, Yorkshire, and Derbyshire, not to speak of Sherwood Forest and Delamere Forest, upon which cultivation has encroached. Stone walls in the north take the place of hedgerows. Streams and rivers run faster than in the south, and are singularly pure until polluted in their course by the refuse of dye-factories, ironworks or drains. The chief trees are fir, pine, and ash: or if the oak grows, it looks gnarled, scrubby, and starved. The birch is fairly common, but the beech and elm seldom occur, and do not reach the size of the southern trees. Probably they suffer more from cold and wind, or from the smoke that blackens and shrivels most trees for miles around the great manufacturing towns, making them look like the woods along the fighting front in France.

The difference of scene in the north inevitably affects the character of the northern people. Many live in rows of cottages along a rocky hillside where in the evening the lights in windows and shops twinkle upon the gloomy slope like illuminated beads upon a purple robe, and they look far below upon the smoking chimneys of the mills where they work all day. The homes of others cluster round the shafts of perilous mines or flaring blast-furnaces. Others, again, huddle in monotonous streets over an extended plain, where one city runs into the next almost without division, and all are damp with rain or the westerly mist upon which their manufactures flourish.

But even from Wigan and Oldham and Manchester the moorlands, fells, and valleys are nowhere far away, and nature has given to the further north a beauty of lake and mountain still secluded and enduring. There indeed the grey or whitewashed farms and the cottages of the shepherds, even more than the cottages of southern villages, seem to have grown out of the earth. They are themselves part of it, and they cling to the hillsides as a pine tree clings with its roots. For the poet of that countryside there

is no need to search and choose. No pastoral poet of swains and nymphs and grots, he was the boy who, rowing on a lake, suddenly saw a peak, black and huge, tower between him and the stars, and like a living thing stride after him as he rowed away:

> "For many days, my brain
> Worked with a dim and undetermined sense
> Of unknown modes of being; o'er my thoughts
> There hung a darkness, call it solitude
> Or blank desertion. No familiar shapes
> Remained, no pleasant images of trees,
> Of sea or sky, no colours of green fields;
> But huge and mighty forms, that do not live
> Like living men, moved slowly through the mind
> By day, and were a trouble to my dreams."[1]

Solemn influences like those work, however unconsciously, upon the souls of grave and lonely dwellers among the hills. It was of those dwellers that the boy in after life told the history, "homely and rude," for the delight of a few natural hearts:

> "And, with yet fonder feeling, for the sake
> Of youthful Poets, who among these Hills
> Will be my second self when I am gone."[2]

There are many who have known themselves to be that second self.

Whether northerners or southerners, we English owe much of our peculiar character to our peculiar climate. We should be a very different people if our

[1] *The Prelude*, Book I.
[2] Wordsworth's *Michael*.

air were as hot as Central Africa's, or as cold as
Spitzbergen's. Sometimes we say it is very hot,
sometimes very cold, but those of us who have
known real heat or real cold do not say so. Profes-
sors of agriculture have told me that England requires rain every day, and if that is true, it is hard
to understand why our farmers grumble. They get
more rain in the north and west than in the eastern
counties, and that difference, no doubt, affects the
temperaments of the people; but the country as a
whole enjoys fairly regular and widely distributed
rain, so that the air is usually full of moisture.
Rivers and brooks seldom run dry — so embarrassing a habit in less happy lands. Thus they serve with
little interruption for drinking, washing, sport, or
drainage, and the proximity of the sea to every part
of the country exercises an incalculable influence
upon the character of our varied race.

The chief interest of our climate is that we can
never tell what is going to happen next. On the same
day we may be driven to sit in the shade and to
light the fire; on the same day we may be stifled by
motionless fog and swept by shrieking gales. Thus
the weather naturally supplies us with the staple
of conversation, just as Prohibition supplies the
Americans. The climate's variety has become part
of our nature. We must hold ourselves ready for
anything, and the readiness is all.

A country so various in scene and sky has, naturally, produced and nurtured a large variety of

living creatures — beasts, birds, and insects. Happily for all of us except sportsmen, the larger beasts
have disappeared, some in prehistoric times, a few
within the last two or three centuries only. There
was a time when mammoths, enormous cave-lions
and cave-bears roamed the icy or tropical scene.
Once when a heavy skull was dug up beneath our
newspaper's office in Fleet Street, I labelled it
" Head of a prehistoric Editor," but I was wrong.
It had belonged to a hippo which once wallowed in
the ouse of a vast river — perhaps one of the rivers
which helped to deposit Holland. Our legends, fairy
tales, and place-names tell of bears, wolves, and
beavers, but I suppose the bears which supplied
sport when baited with dogs, and suggested the apt
comparisons of " sulky as a bear " or " as a bear
with a sore head," were not wild or native. Nor perhaps were the wolves that " wolfed it down," as a
hungry man devours food. I do not know whether
the beavers which gave gentility to hats a century
ago and so propagated the " silk hat," now mori-
bund, were trapped in Yorkshire ; but probably they
were imported by the Hudson's Bay Company.

The few larger quadrupeds remaining are chiefly
preserved in order to be killed for fun. Such are the
red deer, the roe, the fallow deer, and the fox, all
of which would probably have disappeared but for
the pleasure taken in shooting them or chasing them
to death with hounds. Otters are also hunted to
death with a special breed of hounds, but, being

scarcer, are not so frequently slaughtered for sport. Badgers, like bears, may no longer be baited for amusement, but are killed as vermin, or to supply shaving-brushes. Hares and rabbits, besides being shot for food, are also coursed with dogs, chiefly as as occasion for betting.

Hedgehogs are killed as vermin, but sometimes as food. Ferrets are used to draw objects of sport from their holes of refuge. Weasels and stoats are killed as vermin. Rats are killed as vermin, or caged as a poor man's sport for terriers to kill at a penny a head. Mice supply cats with interest and partial nourishment. The wild-cat, the pine-marten, and the polecat have become almost too rare to be counted.

It will be seen that most of our surviving quadrupeds are chiefly beneficial for the pleasure they give us in killing them. The same is true of a good many among our birds, such as the pheasant (perhaps not strictly an English bird, for its name derives from the river Phasis in the Caucasus, where I have seen it in great numbers, though always of the white-ringed variety), the grouse, the partridge, the woodcock, and the snipe. Unlike the fox or the otter, these birds are good to eat, and they are preserved for that reason as well as for the amusement of shooting them. Other largish birds, such as the eagle, the osprey (very scarce in England), the heron, the raven, the various species of owl, the jay, and most of the sea-birds and fresh-water birds, except the ducks, are not killed for food, but because they destroy lambs, grouse, young pheasants, eggs, or fish.

Smaller birds of great variety in plumage and song frequent the English part of the island. Many follow the distinction between north and south; many come only for the spring and summer; a certain number use the land only as a resting place in passage. The nightingale, the lark, the blackbird, and the thrush are most famous for song, and have been most celebrated by our poets. But all, down to the tiny golden-crested wren, have their distinctive notes, and out in the southern counties in May they combine their songs in a " dawn chorus," beginning about an hour before sunrise. The lark, indeed, springs up still earlier — at the first glimmer of daylight — as though to sound his pleasure first, and the comfortable wood-pigeon comes in last. The nightjar or goatsucker has a monotonous but peculiarly beautiful churring song, to which he adds a kind of cymbal by clapping his wings over his back. The corncrake also has a monotonous but less beautiful note, and both are difficult to locate. So is the cuckoo, that " wandering voice " of spring.

All our lakes, ponds, fens, rivers, and streams, except the polluted, abound in coots, moorhens, and dabchicks. Kingfishers have probably increased since the fashion of sticking bits of them in women's hats has passed. The attempts to induce the booming bittern and the crested grebe to return have partially succeeded, but whether the " bird sanctuaries" increase the number of small inland birds is a doubtful question, since their enemies, such as the jay, are there also protected. The coastal sanctuaries, such as the famous one at Scolt Head in Norfolk, appear to be successful, though one might suspect the rare but voracious greater blackback gull as a devourer of the young. But all our shores and estuaries still swarm with sea-birds in spite of oil-fuel flung from ships — gulls of four or five species, cormorants, guillemots, oyster-catchers, redshanks, avocets, dotterel, and sandpipers. For beauty, power of flight, and assured speed in diving, the gannet or solan goose surpasses all, and it is a delight to watch him turn this way and that way before he plunges sheer down below the surface, as no gull can plunge.

Slowworms and small lizards are common on our sandy heaths, when the sun is warm, but we have no poisonous snakes, except the adder or viper, easily distinguished by the beautiful dark-brown, dia-mond-shaped markings on its back. Few of our in-sects are dangerously hurtful, the hornet being the worst, unless we must include the malarial mos-quito, which now rarely occurs, even in the fens. Moths and beetles swarm in copious variety, the most ominous to country people being the death's head moth (a large but harmless insect feeding on the potato plant), and the death-watch beetle (equally harmless except to old timber, but making a click by throwing the thorax back upon the cara-pace, either to turn right way up or to attract the attention of a mate). Our butterflies are of singular beauty, as the peacock, the red admiral, the clouded yellow (with many varieties), the tortoise-shell, and the orange-tip. Some even approach tropical splendour, as the purple emperor, the swallowtail of Wicken fen, the Camberwell beauty (rare and unique, differing in the deeper colour of its border from the Continental variety), and the brilliantly metallic Adonis blue.

It is among all this wealth of animal and insect life that the English people have been bred. The influence of all, as of the trees, plants, and flowers in woods, fields, moors, and hills, is felt in our nature and in our ancient songs. The countless fish in rivers, streams, and sea, are also part of ourselves.

CHAPTER II

THE RACE

"This Happy Breed of Men."
King Richard II, Act II, Scene 1.

Our caricaturists have no difficulty in fixing the type of foreign nations. The mincing Frenchman, the ponderous German, the barbaric Russian, the exuberant Italian, the intrusive American, the fawning Jew — they are all caught, and at once we recognize them all. Yet all are untrue. I could draw equally fair types of the Frenchman as Rabelais, the German as Goethe, the Russian as Tolstoy, the Italian as Dante, the American as Lincoln, the Jew as Heine or Spinoza. As to ourselves, we all know how foreigners depict us — our men with long noses, an eyeglass, enormous check suits, knickerbockers, spindle legs, and a short wooden pipe; our women with projecting teeth, feet like canoes, draggled skirts, and flat frontage. The pictures are untrue, but not more untrue than our own caricature of ourselves — a caricature that we even regard with a certain pride. It is called " John Bull," and it represents a paunchy, aggressive, irascible old farmer in top-boots, white breeches, swallowtail coat, low-crowned hat, and side-whiskers, usually threatening violence with a heavy stick in support of a corpulent female called Britannia. It is a figure never seen in England, and it resembles the average Englishman in no single respect. The strangest thing about it is that the name, and I suppose the ideal, was invented by one of the wits in Queen Anne's reign, when I should have thought such an ideal was peculiarly abhorrent to the elegance of the time.[1] Yet our own caricaturists have used it for many generations as the very type of our racial appearance and temper, thus diffusing among us an impression as false as any that a foreigner's malice could inspire.

Humbert Wolfe, poet and satirist both, has wittily said that M. Maurois in his *Ariel* has described Shelley as a Man about Heaven. Shelley was essentially an Englishman, and M. Maurois's description of him is exact and penetrating, but neither we nor any foreigner would ever think of drawing Englishmen as Men about Heaven. Yet I could argue that the caricature would be just as true as " John Bull."

The more we know, the less we generalize. All mankind, all races, all individual men and women are full of contradictions. But I doubt if the contradictions in any race are so obvious and so perplexing as in the English. I suppose we may attribute

---

[1] *Law* (i.e. War) *is a Bottomless Pit; or the History of John Bull*, probably by John Arbuthnot (1712).

our extreme diversity to the diversity of races from which we have sprung. We need not go back to the neolithic cave-dwellers who disputed the sloughs and forests with mammoths and saurians. It is dangerous to speak even of the dark Iberians, or of the so-called "Celts" who overcame but did not exterminate the Iberians only a few centuries B.C.; for some infuriated professor will bristle at the words. But we may say with assurance that when Cæsar invaded Britain he found it inhabited. For a victorious general and a Roman of his time, his description is unusually ample, and as we must call the people something, I may be excused for keeping the old-fashioned word "Celtic." It and its variations have now served for two thousand years, sometimes for praise, more often for blame. I remember the time when "the Celtic fringe" (Brittany, Cornwall, Wales, the west coast of Scotland and the south and west of Ireland) was spoken of with tolerant contempt. But I also remember the rather later time when the "Celt" was adored as a beautifully imaginative and highly spiritual being to whom everything admirable in our English character and art could be traced, while the heavy "Anglo-Saxon" crept or rumbled in his wake with solid, stolid stupidity.[1]

Though Iberian-Celtic Britain was joined to the

---

[1] Matthew Arnold greatly encouraged this enthusiasm by his Essays on Celtic Literature (1867). But it raged especially during the 'nineties of last century, and was further inspired by the Irish literary movement of those years.

Roman Empire for nearly four hundred years, probably little of the Roman nature has descended to ourselves. Here and there Romans built fine villas and largish towns or fortresses, such as London, Silchester, Leicester, Colchester, Chester, and York. Apart from the prehistoric or Iberian devious roads they also built long straight roads for the march of legions from fortress to fortress. They built the "Hadrian's Wall" from the Solway to the Tyne in the hope of checking the advance of still more barbaric Celts from the north, and under Severus, nearly a century later (about A.D. 210) it was restored and strongly fortified, as we see in its remains to-day. Most of the soldiers were probably British, but many Latin inscriptions prove that officers, sometimes with wives and children, came from Italy, and one can only pity those who were stationed among the desolate moorlands crossed by the Wall, with British Celts behind, and still savager Celts in front. What a life for men and women who had known Rome or Naples!

We also learn from the monuments on the Wall that the Romans brought with them the mystical worship of Mithras who slew the sacred bull. Probably at the same time or but little later the earliest worship of Christ was introduced into the island. But so far as England was concerned, the early British Church was almost if not entirely obliterated after the Roman protection was withdrawn from the country early in the fifth century, and even the tradition of the Roman laws faded away.

In their bloodthirsty invasions the Angles, Saxons, and Jutes (Germans, now classed together with the Danes and other Scandinavians as " Nordic") destroyed the coating of Roman civilization so completely that its remains are now seen merely in traces of amphitheatres, as at Silchester and Dorchester, in a few ancient walls, as at York and Leicester, in baths, as in London and Bath, in one or two basilicas transformed into churches, in the mosaic pavements excavated in many places, and in the thin red tiles built into the walls of later times. But during the invasions, and the struggle of some two hundred subsequent years, it is doubtful how completely the Iberian-Celtic peoples themselves were destroyed together with such Roman civilization as they had acquired. It is unlikely that the invaders, who at first came without their families, should have slaughtered the Celtic women and girls as well as their husbands, sons, and lovers. For Celtic women are so proverbially beautiful and charming that by force or persuasion the intruding warriors would naturally make them mothers who might survive the rude change in their relationships and manner of life.

From this mingling of Iberian, Celt, and Saxon our English race mainly sprang. It has been called a happy breed of men, and so it is; but in most of us there runs a thin strain which does not lead to happiness. A modern poet felt it there when he wrote:

> "When Severn down to Buildwas ran
> Coloured with the death of man,
> Couched upon her brother's grave
> The Saxon got me on the slave.
>
> The sound of fight is silent long
> That began the ancient wrong;
> Long the voice of tears is still
> That wept of old the endless ill.
>
> In my heart it has not died,
> The war that sleeps on Severn side;
> They cease not fighting east and west,
> On the marches of my breast.
>
> Here the truceless armies yet
> Trample, rolled in blood and sweat;
> They kill and kill and never die;
> And I think that each is I." [1]

There we see that division which rends the English soul, disturbs its peace, and torments it with a melancholy yearning for intangible and unattainable visions. Whence come our freaks of genius, and our masters of poetic thought and form, but also the apparently commonplace men who suffer a life of divided aims, uncertain whether fond idealism or material good sense should prevail upon the battlefield of their spirit.

In the first two verses of the same poem one feels in emblem another side of the same perennial

[1] *A Shropshire Lad:* "The Welsh Marches," by A. E. Housman (1896).

struggle — the proud dominance of the Saxon, and
the irresistible beauty of the conquered race:

> " High the vanes of Shrewsbury gleam
>   Islanded in Severn stream;
>   The bridges from the steepled crest
>   Cross the water east and west.
>
> The flag of morn in conqueror's state
>   Enters at the English gate:
>   The vanquished eve, as night prevails,
>   Bleeds upon the road to Wales."

On the whole we may say that the Angles, the
Saxons (if we must keep up the ancient distinction)
and the smaller tribe of Jutes, inhabiting different
parts of the country, formed the basis of the English race, and contributed our main characteristics.
They were good fighters but unmilitary, brutal but
good-tempered, tolerant but religious worshippers
of Thor and Odin. These contradictions were further sharpened by the Iberians and Celts, either in-
terbred with them or hanging on to their borders.
And fresh incitements to activity were added by the
two main inroads of Danes and other Scandinavians, who by degrees occupied almost as much of the
country as their predecessors, and left traces of their
occupation in the names of villages upon the eastern
and midland counties, as well as in the Scandinavian Lake district. The different breeds can still be
easily distinguished by pronunciation and dialect,[1]
but more important than names or dialects is the

[1] See Bernard Shaw's *Pygmalion.*

love of the sea and maritime adventure, combined
with a sharp tang of piracy, which came into our
blood from the Norsemen. Looking at the fishermen
on the beach at Aldeburgh, George Meredith, proud
of his Irish and Welsh ancestry, used to say to me,
" There go pirates of your breed! " He was thinking
of our Empire.

The redeeming influence of the Normans was even
more decisive and more conspicuous until it, too,
was absorbed into the common breed. Though of
Scandinavian stock, they had acquired more civi-
lized qualities during their prolonged settlement in
northwest France, and for about three centuries
after the Conquest they imposed French behaviour
and a kind of French language upon the island
race. Carlyle thus speaks of their service to our
nature:

> "England itself, in foolish quarters of England, still
> howls and execrates lamentably over its William Con-
> queror and rigorous line of Normans and Plantagenets;
> but without them, if you will consider well, what had it
> ever been? A gluttonous race of Jutes and Angles, capable
> of no grand combinations; lumbering about in pot-bellied
> equanimity; not dreaming of heroic toil and silence and
> endurance, such as leads to the high places of this Uni-
> verse, and the golden mountain-tops where dwell the Spir-
> its of the Dawn." [1]

That is only partially true, for even the comfortable Saxon was not likely to lumber about in pot-

---

[1] *Frederick the Great*, Book IV, Chapter 3.

bellied equanimity when surrounded by intermarried relations of Iberian, Celtic, and Scandinavian descent. But still their Norman blood probably gave a certain grace and dignity to the feudal landholders after the Conquest, and certainly it introduced the ornamental ideal of chivalry into the country. Most of this ennobling blood was shed in futile wars for the possession of France, or in internecine strife over the succession of kings to the English throne. But the baronial families set an example of nobility, and even though recruited from the ranks of wealthy bankers, brewers, and newspaper proprietors, the aristocracy have claimed and sometimes displayed a refinement of manners distinct from the habits of the common people. Some writers have even detected a superiority in appearance — taller stature, more dignified carriage, and more distinctive noses, due, no doubt, to copious feeding for several generations. But such claims to a peculiarly aristocratic distinction of type seem to have been most justified in the eighteenth century, when life among the gentlefolk was most elegant, pleasing, and self-satisfied, being entirely free from the social and economic doubts and questionings since so troublesome to the sensitive conscience.

The effect of Norman-French upon our language is even more obvious than are the charming manners of the aristocracy. We habitually talk and write an admixture of German and French, such as constitutes the only peaceful relation between those

conflicting races. The mixture provides so serviceable a flexibility of speech that we can say the same
thing twice over in entirely different words, as was
the habit of Dr. Johnson, and is still the useful resource of our rhetoricians. Besides, owing to this
double origin of language, speakers and writers are
enabled to add to our short, sharp English words
the charm of harmonious resonance and a convenient obscurity of meaning by interspersing Latinized
words, and cadences that undulate with the regularity of oceanic billows.

It accords with our English adoration of tradition that many of our constitutional and statutory
phrases retain the form of Norman-French. We still
speak of *Mortmain;* the assent of the Crown to
Bills in Parliament is still given in the words " *Le
Roi le veult*"; and the royal motto commemorating
the dubious incident that originated the Order of
the Garter is composed in the French of the four-
teenth century. No doubt it is felt that chivalrous
French is most fitly adapted to the queerest Order
in the world; unless, indeed, the Order of the Bath
is queerer still.

To the Norman habit of writing laws and statutes
in Latin we also owe the use of several Latin
phrases still surviving in legal and even ordinary par-
lance; such as *sine die, ipso facto, ab ovo, ultra
vires, ceteris paribus, in loco parentis, mutatis mu-
tandis, et cetera, inter alia, v.,* and *re.* The per-
petuation of these antiquated Latinisms provides

lawyers and municipal clerks with the double advantage of displaying their superior learning and confusing the poor and uneducated in offices and law-courts.

So the influence of our conquest by the Norman-French has been far more vital and lasting than that of the less hostile incursions of Scots under James I and continually since his time, or of the Dutch under William III, or of Germans under George I. But all those three races have exercised some influence upon our national character, chiefly in mitigating the ultra-refinement of our aristocracy, but also in introducing elements of thrift, caution, and material acquisitiveness otherwise foreign to the English nature. Somewhat similar has been the influence of the Jews, who were readmitted to the country by Cromwell after four centuries of exclusion. The Flemings exiled from the Netherlands, and the Huguenots exiled from France brought skilled industries with them, in contrast to grasping aliens from other lands. And when they are taken into some small account, the origins of the confused and self-contradictory English race as we now exist are fairly well enumerated.

CHAPTER III

THE MONARCHY

"Cover your heads and mock not flesh and blood
With solemn reverence: throw away respect,
Tradition, form, and ceremonious duty,
For you have but mistook me all this while:
I live with bread like you, feel want,
Taste grief, need friends."
> *King Richard II,* Act III, Scene 2.

IN HIS acute but friendly analysis of the English
character, Salvador de Madariaga, Professor of
Spanish in Oxford, makes some general observations which we may consider, all the more because
they come from a foreigner. After describing our instinct for action, self-control, and social service, he
continues later in his book:

"No law, no force imposes on the people the carefully
poised hierarchy on which all social life rests. The hierarchy is so naturally accepted that the Englishman is
hardly aware of its existence, and to this day believes himself to be living in the land of equality. . . . The true
category of English life is not equality but liberty. For
liberty is the absence of political constraint, and we know
that political constraint is unnecessary in a people gifted
with a genius for spontaneous organization which puts its
citizens automatically at the disposal of the community."[1]

[1] *Englishmen, Frenchmen, Spaniards,* p. 130 (1928).

In the great Trinity of Liberty, Equality, and
Fraternity, we certainly put Liberty first, though we
prefer to call it Freedom, as implying something
more solid in the hand. Fraternity we pass with an
indulgent smile, as a soft and affected sort of thing.
We suspect a tang of the Continental doctrinaire
lurking in it, so that when we receive a letter signed
"Yours fraternally," we assume a tiresome, well-
intentioned crank, and are sometimes right. We
fondly believe in equality in the eyes of the Law,
and when I was brought before a London magis-
trate side by side with a lady of wealth and position, I was grateful to the equality which discharged us both with a sermon, whereas, if we had
both been equally poor and obscure, we should have
been imprisoned without phrase. But the plea for
equality of property and income so persuasively put
forward by Mr. Bernard Shaw, the wisest of our
foreign critics, slides off the hearts of our intelligent
women as something theoretic and impracticable.[1]

Professor de Madariaga tells us that we find nothing contradictory between the atmosphere of liberty
and our "hierarchical structure." English society,
he says, is not homogeneous, but naturally divided
into classes and sub-classes, each of which plays a
distinct part in the work of the whole.

"Thus the social structure of England may be assimilated" (he means compared) "to a pyramid solidly built

[1] See *The Intelligent Woman's Guide to Socialism and Capitalism*, by
G. Bernard Shaw (1928).

on a wide basis of willing and debonair lower classes, which support a whole system of upper classes gradually tapering as they approach the apex. The apex is the King."

I wish I could find more justification among our lower classes for the epithet "debonair," but we may admit the comparison to a pyramid and its apex.

Royal authority seems to have been derived from the worship of divinity, and next from the primitive father's (some say the mother's) dominance in the family and his defence of its young and feminine members. The very word "King" is said to be connected with parentage (compare the Latin *"gen"* in *"genitive," "genus," "generation,"* and the similar Greek forms). Many races have called their king a "father" of his people, though the Homeric word "shepherd" of his people seems more appropriate. The Russian Tsars were of the kind who chasten those whom they love, but still a Tsar was given the endearing title of "Little Father" as a sign of family affection; and even a Sultan's Turkish name signified the head of the domestic circle. Parents maintain their claim to authority by feeding and protecting their young, restraining them from danger, and beating, pinching, or otherwise giving pain when they disregard the commands of parental wisdom.

Similarly the primeval tribe selected some person conspicuous for courage and skill as their father or king, and the custom became so general that in early times the Jews insisted upon having a king " like all the nations to judge them and fight their battles," thus exercising the two main functions of a father in a family. They demanded a king as a central authority, to escape from the anarchy under which " every man did that which was right in his own eyes." [1] Their religious adviser warned them what would be the result. He told them a king would take their sons and make them his drivers and outrunners, his captains, gleaners, harvesters, and armourers; would take their daughters and make them his confectioners, cooks, and bakers; would take the best of their land, and levy a tithe on the seed and the produce. In spite of these wise and prudent warnings, the Jews insisted, until at last their guide yielded and selected Saul " a choice young man and a goodly," to be King. [2]

In return for his laborious duties of judging and fighting battles, the king from early times enjoyed certain privileges in nearly all nations, such as the use of a fine walking-stick called a sceptre, a fine hat called a crown, a fine seat called a throne, in some countries a fine ball called an orb, and in England a fine crystal coach like Cinderella's. Other symbols of profound respect were formerly usual even after the king's own death, as may be seen in the portentous ornamentation of the royal tombs of Egypt, and in the offerings at the royal burials in Ur of the

---

[1] Judges xxi, 25.   [2] 1 Samuel viii and ix.

Chaldees, where numerous horses, oxen, grooms, guards, and concubines were slaughtered as sacrifices to supply service and pleasure in another world, all the victims, except the quadrupeds, probably regarding such a death as an honour. In the case of our English monarchy, however, many of these privileges have fallen out of use.

Within living memory the virtues of a Queen's Consort, hated and despised during his life as a musical and artistic foreigner, were celebrated after his death by a large music hall and the Albert Memorial in Kensington Gardens. The funerals of Queen Victoria and her son King Edward were conducted with military pomp, and attended by Continental kings and emperors, of whom there were more in those days than now. Two, or, counting Holyrood (where an ex-miner and his wife, an ex-mill hand, now, in 1930, represent Royalty), three Royal Palaces are still maintained, and two country seats; but one seaside residence has been abandoned. In former times one king would call himself "France," another "Spain," another "England," and when Louis XIV exclaimed "The State? I am the State!" he was not confined as a maniac. But I doubt if our present King would speak of himself as "England." Technically, I believe he is "His Britannic Majesty," but usually "King of England" or, in India, "The King-Emperor," a title devised by Disraeli for Queen Victoria with ingratiating flattery and Imperial foresight. But even now the English King speaks in state of "My Navy," "My Army," and "My Government." For, as the observant Spaniard says, our King is the apex of the State's pyramid; and we may add, of the Empire's pyramid too. General Smuts, at all events, also an acute foreign observer, during his visit to England and the United States in 1929 dwelt with insistence upon the service of the Crown as supplying the highest point or apex to which all the Dominions could look up with a sense of unity with each other and with the old country too.

From the time of the Great Charter onwards the actual powers of the Monarchy have been gradually reduced, sometimes by violence, sometimes by documents, more often by lapse of time. The idea of absolutism either in Church or State, or in a Monarch who embodies Church and State, as our Monarch constitutionally does, is abhorrent to the English nature. The Englishman is intensely individualist. It has been well said that every Englishman is at heart an anarchist. It is true that the most logical claim for the omnipotence of the State was enunciated by an Englishman, Thomas Hobbes of Malmesbury, under the similitude of the Leviathan or "mortal God." "Without a State," he wrote, "the life of man is solitary, poor, nasty, brutish, and short," and the preservation of the State is of more importance than the freedom of the individual.

"Loss of liberty is really no inconvenience, for it is the only means by which we have any possibility of preserving

ourselves. For if every man were allowed the liberty of
following his own conscience, in such differences of con-
sciences, they would not live together in peace an hour."

Writing in the age of the Civil War, he was so ter-
rified of rebellion against the State that, probably
having Plutarch's *Lives* in mind, he forbade the
reading of Greek and Roman history—"which
venom I will not doubt to compare to the biting of a
mad dog." And on rebels he would have no mercy:

> "On rebels vengeance is lawfully executed, not only to
> the fathers, but also to the third and fourth generations
> not yet in being, and consequently innocent of the fact
> for which they are afflicted."[1]

Yet even Hobbes made some attempt to establish
his Leviathan upon an imaginary consent of all citizens; for in his main definition he says:

> "The Covenant of the State is made in such a manner
> as if every man should say to every man: 'I authorize and
> give up my right of governing myself to this man, or to this
> assembly of men, on this condition that thou give up thy
> right to him and authorize all his actions in like manner.'
> This done, the multitude so united is called a Common-
> wealth, in Latin Civitas. This is the generation of that
> great Leviathan, that mortal God, to whom we owe, under
> the immortal God, our peace and defence."

It may be said that by the Suffrage, which at last
in 1918 became general for nearly all grown-up men
and women, except peers, criminals, and lunatics,
the English do so far as possible comply with the

[1] *De Corpore Politico*, II.

terms of this Covenant, and so put themselves under the control of the State. But in both religious and political life, our history has been marked by repeated and often successful endeavours to escape from external authority, and, though Hobbes was English and Nietzsche was a German, an Englishman's attitude to the State is better expressed by the foreigner's Zarathustra, where he says:

"The coldest of all cold monsters is called the State. Coldly it utters its lies, and this lie crawls from its mouth: 'I, the State, am the people.'

"Destroyers lay snares for the multitude, and call it the State. They dangle above the people a sword and a thousand vain desires.

"Where there is still a people, it does not comprehend the State, but hates it as the evil eye and as a sin against habits and rights.

"Every people speaks its own language of good and evil, which its neighbour does not understand. In its habits and rights it discovered its own tongue.

"But the State lies about good and evil in all languages. Whatever it says is a lie, and whatever it owns it has stolen." [1]

Considering our racial attitude towards external authority, we have been fortunate in our Royal Families, and the Royal Families have been fortunate too. With few exceptions, such as Henry II, Edward I, and perhaps Elizabeth, our Kings and Queens have not been abnormally clever or dominating; nor, with few exceptions, have they been

[1] *"Also sprach Zarathustra," Kap. "Vom neuen Götzen."*

abnormally ill-behaved. When a king seemed bent upon upsetting the habits of our unwritten Constitution, the class in power killed him, acting as the French and Russians did in similar cases. When his son seemed bent upon upsetting the habitual form of religion, they deposed and exiled him, excluding even his posterity from the realm. But as a rule members of the Royal Family have been well treated, except by other members of their own stock who indulged in family quarrels for the dubious advantages of succession to the throne.

For the last century our good fortune in monarchy has, indeed, been remarkable. Succeeding a simple-minded king, whose dullness was varied only by insanity; a detested debauchee, whose feeling was petrified by excess; and a person of no importance, the youthful Queen Victoria restored a waning respect for Royalty by her innocence, her decent behaviour, general good sense, occasional flashes of genius, and the rapid growth of her family. This respect she gradually increased by profound mourning for her Consort, by living to a great age, arranging suitable marriages for her sons and daughters among the kindred Royal Houses of Germany, and by bestowing her confidence upon a singularly fascinating and imaginative Prime Minister of Jewish origin, though she maintained a marked hostility towards an English statesman who possessed every fascinating power but flattery.

Unhappily for her successor, his mother's

dominance overshadowed him so long that his chance of revealing his powers came to him almost too late in life.[1] He was a man of thwarted energy, resolved to play a leading part in Continental diplomacy. Perhaps it was a dangerous part, for it is doubtful whether his activities in regard to France and Russia did not conduce to the World War. But certainly he endeared himself to a large section of the English people simply by a reaction from his mother's secluded and abstemious life. The wealthy and speculative classes admired him as a type of character easy and pleasant for wealthy and speculative people to imitate. All but the diminishing number of the austere regarded him with sympathetic condonation as a sportsman, a sociable fellow, and one who openly enjoyed God's good gifts without puritanic reservations. Even among the stricter members of the middle classes, who had gravely condemned certain youthful extravagances, his providential recovery from a serious illness at the age of thirty was regarded as a reassurance of virtue, and throughout his brief reign he remained one of the most popular of kings.

His son, our present King George V, during the war with Germany made the patriotic mistake of changing the historic family name of Guelph for the lodging-house name of Windsor, but one may say that, in a reign now becoming long, he has fulfilled the duties demanded of his position with quiet com-

[1] See *The Tragedy of Edward VII*, by W. H. Edwards (1928).

mon sense and unflagging industry. Like his father
he greatly enhanced his popularity by surviving a
dangerous illness (1929), and in ordinary life his
labours are neither light nor pleasant. For more than
two hundred years the King has ceased to preside at
Cabinet meetings, and though he may possess the
right of veto, it is not exercised, though sometimes
threatened. A learned German Professor tells us
that "The King has, in the course of time, sunk
from being the most important to the least important factor in legislation." [1] That is, no doubt, true
in regard to actual legislation, but Professor Dibelius goes on to say:

> "The King's opinion is of importance to the leading
> statesman. It will penetrate through countless channels
> into Court and aristocratic circles and the political Clubs.
> The opinion of the Sovereign — when the throne is occu-
> pied by a personality, like Victoria or Edward VII, who
> refuses to be gagged by the convenient theory that the
> King can communicate only with the Prime Minister — is
> bound to be one of the factors with which the Prime Min-
> ister has got to reckon. This is notably, but by no means
> exclusively, the case in relation to questions of foreign
> policy."

As an instance of a King's influence in foreign
politics, I may quote a small experience of my own.
When in Russia during the revolutionary months of
1905–1906, I heard on high military authority that
two Russian army corps were being organized on the

[1] *England*, by Wilhelm Dibelius, Professor of English at Berlin University; p. 228.

frontiers of Finland for the reconquest of that Imperial Duchy. On my return to London, early in 1906, I was invited through the Prime Minister's (Sir Henry Campbell-Bannerman's) secretaries to give the information to King Edward. Having been escorted into Buckingham Palace, I told what I knew to an equerry, who ran to and fro between me and His Majesty, bearing questions and answers from one room to the next. At last the equerry stood still and said, "The King asks if there is anything further you would wish to say," and I replied: "I should like to ask the King to write a personal letter to the Tsar warning him that if he wishes to conclude the proposed agreement with the English people, as I believe the King also desires, the invasion of England with two Russian army corps would be a bad beginning." Away trotted the equerry, and on returning he said, "The King cannot make any such promise, as it would be interfering with the affairs of a friendly Power, but he thanks you for your information."

About a fortnight later I heard that the Russian army corps had been withdrawn. Of course I cannot be sure that the withdrawal was due to King Edward's representation, but I think it likely.

Even apart from the Royal influence upon foreign relations, which were more vital in the old days of relationships with "superfluous kings," the people expect from the English king the fulfilment of certain functions in which he represents them as a whole. For this purpose great industry is required. "Uneasy lies the head," and when during the Great War in France it was the duty of us war correspondents to attend the King in succession day by day upon his drives near the front, we always found that he had been up and at work by six o'clock in the morning, reading and signing documents of State. It is the King's duty to receive Ministers of divergent views and varied character, maintaining, as far as possible, a polite and equable temper with each; to suggest to them possibilities of agreement and compromise either with the Opposition or with himself; at the opening of Parliament to wear the old-fashioned robes, and to read aloud a speech written for him by the Ministers, sometimes in execrable English; on great occasions to lay foundation stones, to christen battleships, to give his patronage and blessing to public institutions, to visit the Royal Academy, and now and again to deliver tactful addresses, all the more irritating a task if the addresses are not his own composition. An English King's popularity and reputation are also incalculably increased if he enjoys life in the country, keeps racehorses and pedigree bulls, is a good sportsman, likes watching football matches, and displays skill and courage in killing birds and wild beasts. Success in all these strenuous occupations involves ceaseless industry and a notable variety of talent.

The King's subtle but widespread influence upon Society and all social behaviour must also be taken into account. This has not escaped the notice of the German Professor already quoted:

> "Any social group or individual," writes Professor Dibelius, "whom the King distinguishes with his notice receives thereby a social *cachet* that disarms all criticism in the country of Snobbery. . . . In a country which puts less emphasis on the passing of examinations or the possession of knowledge than on bank balance, pedigree, and social connexions, a Royal invitation to Sandringham or Osborne gives a social *cachet* that really means more than even the ownership of millions." [1]

Put Windsor for Osborne, and the eulogy remains true. It is remarkable how many industrious and deserving upstarts strain their ambition to snatch at the skirts of Court life. For example, as is well known, the Royal Garden Parties in Buckingham Palace are open to guests inscribed upon a widely tolerant list. I have seen even literary men and artists invited. I have known yet more who flaunted their invitations with ill-concealed self-satisfaction, and some few who openly showed themselves embittered by exclusion.

The social influence of Royalty is, indeed, subtle and widespread. The characters and habits of the King and the Royal Family exert this influence in many unsuspected but vital directions. For instance, at a public meeting to oppose the sport of fox-hunting, I have heard a speaker charged with disloyalty, almost with profanity, on the ground that

[1] *England*, p. 230.

the Prince of Wales liked to pursue foxes. And when the same Prince once (by a deplorable oversight) appeared in a long dress-coat and turned-up trousers, the fashionable tailors shook their heads in dismay, but admitted that the Prince could set what fashion he pleased.

An even more serious instance of Royal power is given in a passage that appeared in one of our best and most influential papers while the Irish question was still a dominating difficulty for the English Government. I give parts of the whole message as displaying English characteristics in other respects as well. The *Spectator* of July 25, 1903, made the following proposals for remedial measures in the distressful country:

"The Celtic Irish have never, owing to their want of minerals, been able to share fully in the solid wealth of Britain. Their island, though beautiful, has never attracted the sportsman and the tourist, who every year carry so large an income to the happy kingdom north of the Tweed, where even the foibles of the people are just the foibles Englishmen comprehend, and therefore forgive.

"Much of all this it is impossible to alter, as impossible as to change a pasture into a mine by merely desiring the alteration; but something can be done which is worth doing. The Court can visit Ireland.

"Crowds will flock where the King has found it pleasant to live, crowds whose wealth, if it does not exactly fertilize as a new trade would, still produces variety, excitement, a break in that melancholy monotony of which the Irishman through all his literature is so apt to complain, as one of the evils to which he is unjustly subjected."

In that passage one may find a certain type of the English spirit in benevolent, healthy, and full-blown perfection. By this spirit we are taught to see a country's greatest happiness in coal-pits and iron-foundries, or, failing them, in rich visitors who will convert the Irish peasantry into game-keepers, gillies, and caddies. And, next to pits and parasites, this exponent of the English spirit would like to see a Royal Court, which is to be desired because it would attract crowds whose wealth would produce variety, excitement, and a break in that melancholy monotony — and so on. It is true that he thinks the Court would not exactly fertilize as a new trade would, but he places it a good second.

When I was young, a considerable political party, led by Sir Charles Dilke and Mr. Joseph Chamberlain, aimed at the abolition of the Monarchy, and so late as the 'eighties, if an advanced audience went sleepy, one could at once rouse them by shouting for a Republic. Where is that party now? For nearly fifty years I have not heard of it. Good-humoured respect for the Royal Family has wiped the party out, and questions of more tangible importance in the daily life of the working people have taken the place of republicanism. Merely constitutional re-arrangements are felt not to matter very much in comparison with food and shelter. And after all, the process of electing Presidents in other countries does not encourage us to follow their example. The natural succession of an eldest son costs one sick but happy woman a deal of anxiety and pain. It may even cost her life. But take the greatest of Republics, and think what the succession of an American President every four years costs that country in uncertainty, in rhetoric, in expense, in shouting, in sweat, and perhaps in more secretive energies and arts!

So far as I can judge, there is now no desire among the English people to overthrow the Monarchy, and I doubt if a Socialist Revolution would even take the trouble to do it. When the King appears at a Final of the Cup Tie, 90,000 of his subjects rise and cheer as one man. Or consider the wide popularity of the Royal Family's photographs — pictures of the King out shooting, or of the Prince of Wales falling off his horse, of the Duke of Connaught reviewing troops, or, best of all, of the Princess Elizabeth in her perambulator or stroking a puppy-dog! Delight in such photos might be attributed to the snobbery of which we are so often accused, but it would be more gracious to put it down to kindly sympathy with family affection. When just after the Armistice in 1918 the general election was run on the cries of "Hang the Kaiser!" and "Make the Germans Pay!" I was still in Cologne, and anxious Germans asked me whether their former War-Lord would really be hanged, and how much they would have to pay. I told them I couldn't tell what the payment exacted from their misery might come to, but as to hanging the Kaiser, I laughed. He was first-cousin to our gracious Sovereign Lord, the King!

In addition to his secular and civil duties, one must remember that the King is also supreme head of the English Church. The Bidding Prayer recited by the select preacher every Sunday in the University church of Oxford declares the King or Queen to be " in all matters ecclesiastical as well as civil within these his (or her) dominions supreme." While attending those sermons, I used to notice that the preacher, according to his opinions of Church Government, distinctly enunciated or slurred over those words, thus perpetuating the ancient struggle in this country between Church and Crown. The refusal of the Crown, supported in this respect by popular feeling, to submit to the domination or interference of the Church can be traced from early times — even earlier than the notorious breach during the reign of Henry II. The refusal was all the more resolute seeing that the head of the Church was, with one exception, a foreigner living in a foreign Court far away in Rome. It was naturally strengthened during the three generations when rival Popes claimed clerical allegiance, one in Rome and one at Avignon. And it was made final by the Act of Supremacy passed by Henry VIII's Reformation Parliament in 1534. In this Act, Henry, though not strictly speaking a spiritual guide, was styled "the only Supreme Head in Earth of the Church of England called *Anglicana Ecclesia.*"

By the authority of this Statute the King, as *Summus Episcopus*, still nominates the two Archbishops, the Bishops, and Suffragans, the Deans, and many Canons, though I believe, none of the Minor Canons, who are selected chiefly for their musical voices, of which the Monarch is not necessarily a judge. Even in regard to more spiritual capacities, the King does not usually now make the choice according to his own religious convictions, but calls the Prime Minister to his assistance, even though the Prime Minister may not be a member of the Church of England, but a Scottish Presbyterian or a Welsh Nonconformist. This employment of a deputy for spiritual appointments conduces to the Monarch's peace of mind. The Archbishops and Bishops, it is true, after combined prayer for heavenly guidance, invariably find that heavenly guidance confirms the choice of the Supreme Head of the Church.

But this practical and satisfactory arrangement represents, I suppose, the sole remnant of the divinity embodied in a King's person — the divinity that doth hedge a King — which can be traced to prehistoric times, to Athenian, Spartan, and Roman usage, and is still adherent in the chieftains of barbaric tribes. How far it may be regarded as a relic of the Divine Right of Kings over which our ancestors contended so bitterly, it would take long to inquire. But there can be no doubt that the King escapes perturbation by deputing such divine power as he may possess; for even the nominees of his deputies, such as the Archbishops, appear to find some of their divine duties harassing and laborious undertakings.

Note. — The whole question of Monarchy, whether Kingship is held by Divine Right, and whether the King's power should dominate the people, is discussed in " *Vindiciæ contra Tyrannos;* A Defence of Liberty against Tyrants, or Of the lawful power of the Prince over the People, and of the People over the Prince, Being a Treatise written in Latin and French by Junius Brutus, and translated out of Both into English." London, 1689.

In a Historical Introduction to the edition of 1924, Professor Harold Laski discourses at length upon the whole subject of the work, which he inclines to think was written by Duplessis-Mornay, probably between 1574 and 1576. He puts the original publication at 1579. It is remarkable how closely the Frenchman's theoretic conceptions, though largely founded upon Scriptural teaching and example, coincide with contemporary and subsequent practice in England.

CHAPTER IV

THE NOBILITY

"Spacious in the possession of dirt."
Hamlet, Act V, Scene 2.

IN THAT sharp-edged book by Professor de Madariaga, already referred to, we read that the norm
of English society is the aristocrat:

> "This appreciation of the aristocrat may be foolish or
> enlightened, deep or superficial, frank or shamefaced, con-
> scious or sub-conscious, but it is well-nigh universal in
> England. For the aristocrat incarnates the perfect man of
> action and the perfect leader. He is a representative in-
> dividual, for he has power, but he is also a representative
> community type, for he has tradition and he embodies
> leadership. He thus combines in his personality the sense
> of action and the group sense, which are the two dominant
> forces in the English character." [1]

Such a passage may well soothe the spirit of a
Duke, Marquess, Earl, Viscount, or mere Baron as
he walks into the House of Lords, wondering
whether his Order in the country is reality or dream.
From time to time he may have heard wild talk of
mending or ending the House of Lords. A tiresome

[1] *Englishmen, Frenchmen, Spaniards,* p. 129.

writing-fellow, called John Morley, used to talk like that, but in the end he became a Lord himself; so all was well. And now as the aristocrat passes into his appropriate House, leaving those fusty Commons on his left, I hope he is conscious that he incarnates the perfect man of action and the perfect leader. He has power; he has tradition. He is a representative individual; he embodies leadership. He combines the two dominant forces in the English character, and I try to realize all that this implies as I watch him entering the Gilded Chamber, there to listen to the murmured observations of his peers. I try to imagine how ennobling that description would be if only it were realized in myself.

The Peer whom I picture as entering his House of Legislature counts, it is true, but as one among many, so far as his natural powers of action and leadership go. Including Royalty, there are, I believe, nearly thirty Dukes, about as many Marquesses, a good lot of Earls and Viscounts, and quite a crowd of Barons. There are besides a number of full-fledged Bishops, who sit together like a flock of white doves or gulls for the protection of religion and morality. So that the Chamber (rather obscurely known in the House of Commons as "another place") would be uncomfortably crowded if all the Peers and Bishops occupied their seats at the same time. But that excess of zeal is seldom called for. There is no need for Whips, since a sufficient Conservative majority can always be counted upon

to uphold the bulwarks of the Constitution. Liberal Peers are few, and though Labour Peers do now exist, they may feel a little astonished at their presence there, even though they have never belonged to the working classes — astonished as a native oyster which has developed a pearl in his shell.

If opposed by a Liberal or Labour demand violently urged upon them in the country, the Lords have hitherto had recourse to a tactful retreat. But, except in the case of Bills declared by the Speaker to be money-bills, their veto upon the proposals of the House of Commons is absolute, unless the proposal is sent up to them for two years in succession. In that case it is sure to be an advanced proposal, and in two years there is always a good chance that a Labour or Liberal Government may be thrown out of office and the danger overpassed.

Considering their influence upon legislation, and their power in thus averting fresh evil from the country, the Litany in the Book of Common Prayer naturally beseeches God that it may please Him to endue the Lords of the Council, and all the Nobility with grace, wisdom, and understanding, whereas no such prayer in the Litany is regarded as needful for the House of Commons. Yet the Lords, though thus prayerfully endued with grace, wisdom, and understanding, appear to justify their high position by their earthly possessions rather than by those desirable qualities. And the most highly valued of earthly possessions has hitherto been land. Rank among the nobility is generally proportionate to the ownership of land, and the aristocrats in books of reference record in noble rivalry the thousands of acres that they own. So it is that among people of title we must draw an important distinction between the large landowners, who are the aristocrats proper, and others who possess titles but not much land. In the House of Lords one may now indeed discover Peers whose holding in land hardly extends beyond the boundaries of a week-end cottage, and that perhaps only held on lease or rent. Among the Peers of still lesser rank and influence may be included those upon whom titles have been bestowed by the King for special eminence in the country's service at home or abroad — in war, politics, law, or beneficent gifts to the nation. To a similar class belong the Peers distinguished in manufacture, speculation, contribution to Party funds, the ownership of popular newspapers on the Conservative side, and, once or twice a century, in literature, art, or science.

If a title is hereditary, it is thought advisable to bestow it upon candidates without male heirs, lest the House of Lords should become overstocked and flushed with new blood. The title of baronet, however, though hereditary, may be bestowed without apprehension, since baronets do not sit with Lords. And the title of Knight, not being hereditary, may be lavished almost at random, as happened when services in the Great War, including those rendered at a safe and comfortable distance from the front, were copiously rewarded with Knighthoods of the British Empire. These, however, need not be reckoned among the subject of this chapter, nor need the lesser Orders not involving the prefix " Sir."

The landowners who before the Great War possessed a large proportion, perhaps more than half, of the country's surface, had in some few cases inherited their ownership from feudal ancestors to whom the land, nominally in Norman times possessed by the Crown, was granted in return for definite services, especially in war. But most of the feudal families wiped each other out in Royal or personal quarrels before the beginning of the sixteenth century and a new set of big landowners was created by Royal grants or the pillage of the Church and monastic properties during the Reformation. This pillage accounts for the name " Abbey " frequently still attached to the residences of the aristocracy. Sometimes, indeed, the actual ruins of an ancient abbey stand as elegant ornaments in the grounds or park, and have served as a quarry for building the nobleman's present habitation, which, in spite of its name and history, is no longer consecrated to definitely religious or ecclesiastical use.

The area of the landed estates, whether feudal or ecclesiastical in origin, was largely increased during the eighteenth and early nineteenth centuries by the further pillage of Common Lands from the poor, who had used the commons for plough, pasturage, wooding, and recreation from time immemorial.[1] Owing to the absence of title-deeds or to the terror of "the Family" among the cottagers and small-holders, this pillage is still continued by landowners, who from time to time quietly lay barbed wire across the ancient pathways over their pillaged or inherited lands. The original excuses of the land-owners, supported by the economists of last century, were that private property in land was more productive of food for the country than common land could be, and also that it encouraged industry among peasants whom independence made lazy. But though pheasants and other game may fairly be regarded as food by landowners and poachers, these excuses are no longer relied upon. All foreigners charge the English with hypocrisy, but the abandonment of the pleas for pillage seems to prove that the limits of passable hypocrisy may sometimes be reached.

The wealth derived from large estates is evidently diminishing, except in cases where the aristocrat has chanced to own a surface with lucrative mines beneath it, from which he can exact a royalty of so much per ton without effort or expenditure on his part; or except where the surface of his land is in proximity to a developing industrial town, from the ground-rents of which he can exact the "unearned increment," also without effort or expenditure on

[1] It is estimated that at least 20 per cent of the total acreage of England was thus enclosed by landowners at that period. See *The Village Labourer*, by J. L. and Barbara Hammond, Chapters I to IV.

his part. Even where these two casual advantages may be absent, the aristocratic landowner can derive pleasure, not only from sport and social prestige, but from a dominant control over the religious and political opinions of his tenantry. For the pleasure of this control is readily maintained by threat of exile from farm or cottage. A careful landowner may also ensure the control of population by refusing to allow new cottages to be built if they would detract from his game-preserves or the amenity of his pleasure-grounds, and he can limit food-production by refusing small-holdings. A praiseworthy habit of restraint in word and deed is thus impressed upon the countryside, and the fear of the landlord is the beginning of wisdom. This wholesome fear is supported in nearly all country districts by the spiritual influence of the clergy. For the landowner is usually the chief supporter of the Church, perhaps because he appreciates his debt to the divinely clerical association from which he may have derived his property; but more likely because he feels that the attendance of "the poor" at the church services will confirm the stability of the society which keeps him where he is, endued with power and proper respect, as well as with the grace, wisdom, and understanding which for him we pray.

No doubt the old feudal barons, with their shining armour, gorgeous banners, and dominating castles, enjoyed an energetic and boisterous existence, but the typical English aristocracy had their finest time in the eighteenth century. Their manner of life was then elegant, unruffled, unquestioned. Their houses were dignified and commodious, their furniture the most exquisite ever designed, their dress becoming and convenient, their tenants submissive, their servants obedient and plentiful, their wives, horses, and dogs beautiful and well-bred. Their natural claim to the government of the country in peace and war remained undisputed and profitable. By adroit intermarriage or the tenure of political or military office their landed estates might be indefinitely extended, and if they pursued the charms of the fair or the good things of this life with enviable vitality, the clergy attached to their domain did not question their right to high-born behaviour, and the moral teaching of excitable Wesleyans was respectfully limited to the lower orders. In Handel's church at Little Stanmore, near Edgeware, an inscription upon the sculptured marble tomb of a Countess describes her as "the chaste partner of her husband's heart and bed; religious without enthusiasm."

The claim of the aristocracy to high positions in the Foreign Office and the Diplomatic Service is recognized to this day. A list drawn up of the men employed in those services between 1851 and 1929 shows that out of 57 Foreign Office men 17 belonged to the aristocracy with hereditary titles, and out of 210 in the Diplomatic Service 82 belonged to that class also. Out of the combined Services 53 per cent belonged to the aristocracy and gentry (smaller landowners), 22 per cent were sons of professional men, and 4 per cent came from business families. The great majority (240 out of 249) had been at Public Schools.[1] The aristocracy have owed these privileges partly to their wealth and the titles which conduce to influence in Society, thus opening to younger sons a career and a competency. For owing to the old law of primogeniture, the large estates have been till recently held undivided, and something had to be done for younger sons. Even Lord Salisbury, for instance, afterwards Foreign Secretary and Prime Minister, was driven while he was a younger son to the homely, slighted trade of journalist for want of the nobler occupation with which his family should naturally have provided him.

But we may admit finer motives for their public service than the stress of penury or boredom. Generations of outdoor life and plentiful food have given many of the aristocrats a healthy physique, a handsome face, with strongly marked features, and an abundant vitality which demands a wider mental satisfaction than hunting and shooting can give. Many have followed the principle of *Noblesse Oblige*, and undertaken public duties involving work and even hardship. They have acted thus, not merely as making some return for the good fortune and comfort with which the country has supplied them, but because it was expected of them by the

[1] See detailed statistics in the Fabian Tract, by Robert Nightingale (1930).

English tradition. Lord Curzon, for instance, afterwards Viceroy of India and Foreign Secretary, disappeared into unvisited regions of Asia, exposed himself to perils and laboured incessantly throughout life for the good of his country; that is to say, for the good of millions whose existence he ignored or regretted. How happy Sir Edward Grey (Lord Grey) would have been living peacefully among fishes and birds had not the feeling of *Noblesse Oblige* driven him into the turbulent waters of European contention! Lord Grey, it is true, did not spring from an ancestry of large landowners with high-sounding titles, but take the Cecils; what bishops, not only one brother, but all four would have made but for the tradition of Hatfield in political life!

Carlyle thought the aristocracy worth preserving for their good manners. He even looked to them for leadership on that account, though perhaps he would not have selected the most elegant saloon passenger to command a liner in a storm. And it might be objected that it is no hard task to possess good manners when "The Family" has rested on the top of Society and been given all it wanted in the way of food, drink, and shelter for two or three centuries; just as it was easy for the Turk to pose as "the gentleman of the Near East" when for generations he alone had been privileged to carry sword and gun. But still, there, as I am told, the good manners are, and I willingly admit their national value.

For good manners are founded upon the powers of silence and self-control, qualities of inestimable worth. I love to hear a member of our aristocracy opening a flower show or giving away the prizes in a competition for milch cows. His hesitations, his repetitions, his pauses, his tattered *clichés* fill me with delight; for in them I recognize the sterling qualities of my countrymen. And how often among voluble and gesticulating nations I have blessed our aristocracy for their silent restraint of emotion — for that repose which stamps the caste of Vere de Vere. In an entry from the Diary of a German diplomatist, Baron Philipp von Neumann (May 13, 1822), I read:

> "Dined with M. de Chateaubriand. Up to now I have not been able to estimate his character accurately. He has a formal air, is little at his ease, and rather surprised that he is not made as much of here as in Paris, where three duchesses were so much in love with him that one died, another went mad, and the third lost her appetite."[1]

I am confident that if those three admirers of the foreign writer had been English duchesses, they would have contrived to conceal their passions with better success.

Aristocrats have also served the country in more tangible ways, especially by purchasing marbles and paintings from Italy or Holland when works of art went cheap, and by selling them recently at enormous profit, in the hope of diffusing culture in this

[1] Quoted in *The Times* of September 21, 1928.

country and initiating it in the United States. Many
have also collected large libraries, in which the
rows of eighteenth-century volumes are exquisitely
bound and so unreadable that their regularity need
never be disturbed. Others used to build little chap-
els within their grounds or just beyond the park
palings where, in a comfortable square pew warmed
by a stove in the centre, they might on Sunday
morning submit to the wholesome and appetizing
penance of Divine Service, and so encourage the
tenantry to do the same. In more recent times they
have rather chosen to display benevolence by building Workmen's Clubs and patronizing Women's
Institutes. They thus justify the contention of
John Locke that the only right to property is use,[1]
and assuage the village Hampden's dauntless
breast.

That reference suggests "the little tyrant of his
fields," and the tyranny is often baleful. But none
the less, the English aristocrat is not as a rule detested, and his tyranny can hardly be so obnoxious
as was that of the French or Russian landowners before the revolutions in those countries. It may be
that as Professor de Madariaga said, the aristocrat
is "the norm of English Society," and so the normal
mind likes to see him there. At all events the weekly
illustrated papers give us even more numerous pictures of the aristocracy than of the Royal Family,
partly because there are more of them. Photographs

[1] *On Civil Government*, Chap. VI.

of "The Charming Countess of X. off to the Derby," or "The Lovely Lady Y. with her sweet little twins and Pekinese," are evidently very pleasing to the normal mind. For editors are not fools, and their shareholders look for dividends. Descriptions of diamond tiaras, ropes of pearls, and emeralds "big as pigeons' eggs" are also eagerly perused, even when the reader's contact with jewels is limited to Woolworth's sixpenny resemblances.

> "On her white breast a sparkling cross she wore
> Which Jews might kiss and Infidels adore."

So sang Pope of the exquisite Belinda, and people like to hear about such adornments, even when the wearer is less exquisite. Most of us enjoy a fairy story or a pantomime which removes us into a magic land of splendour so different from our homes, and to us the aristocracy supply a vision of gorgeous life more attractive than a pantomime or fairy tale, because it is real. Perhaps for these reasons even country people still retain a reverence, almost an affection, for "The Family" which has occupied the Hall for many generations, and seldom wish to abolish them by murder, arson, execution, or exile, such as has befallen the nobility in less kindly lands. If, as often happens now, the Family is compelled by extravagance or taxation to let or sell the Hall to upstart plutocrats, and reside in some neighbouring villa or lodge, it still remains "The Family" to the village mind, and the villagers have no high opinion of the new-comers, no matter how glaringly they may flaunt their splendour.

But in any case the glory of the aristocratic families as big landowners is departing. The inheritance duties ordained by the Gladstone budget of 1853, and increased by the Lloyd George budget of 1909; the attempts to promote Agricultural Labourers' Unions and strikes by Joseph Arch in the 'sixties and 'seventies of last century; the deaths of sons and heirs in the Great War; the heavy death-duties and enormous taxation still imposed to pay for our victory; have all contributed to the break-up of many large estates and the ruin of ancient families who had neither the unearned increment of urban property nor the sale of valuable works of art to maintain their former incomes and brilliant manner of life. Large estates have changed hands or been divided. Ever since the Armistice the back page of *The Times* has been adorned with alluring pictures of noble mansions and parks now offered for sale. A great proportion of the surface of our country has been alienated from the hereditary owners, and country life, as the aristocracy knew it even twenty or thirty years ago, is rapidly dying out. Great country houses, called mansions or seats as though eternal as the heavens, are fast being converted into residential hotels, clubs, public schools, sanatoriums, or asylums — objects for which in many cases no great change was required. No other country possessed coverts for pleasant and charm-

ing life to compare with our aristocratic houses, and
it is with some regret that we now see them being
diverted to useful purposes. Matthew Arnold condemned them as "The great fortified posts of the
barbarians,"[1] and I am perhaps too prone to the
pleasures of barbaric life — its healthiness, freedom,
good-temper, and close contact with nature. In any
case, I regret the dignified beauty of the old houses
themselves, whether Elizabethan, Queen Anne, or
Georgian. It is unreasonable, but their conversion
into public institutions or mad-houses seems to
diminish their ancient charm; and, though utility
gains, it is no satisfaction to me to meet a schoolmaster or a keeper of lunatics wandering in the
park rather than a shepherd or a keeper of March
hares.

And it is not only from the country that the
abodes of aristocracy are disappearing. Where now
is Devonshire House, Grosvenor House, or Dorchester House? Stafford House and Hertford House are
stuffed with curiosities for the public gaze. Lans-
downe House is being gutted as I write (March,
1930). If, as we are told, the English aristocrat embodies leadership, our leaders must find new shel-
ters to protect them from the weather.

[1] *Culture and Anarchy*, Chapter 3.

CHAPTER V

THE UPPER CLASSES

"The true heroick English gentleman hath no peer."
Sir Thomas Browne in *Christian Morals.*

I. THE GENTRY.

THOUGH THE barrier may be crossed by association in sport and even by intermarriage, the
gentry are distinct from the caste of the aristocracy.
People of the countryside would not speak of the
ranks between Dukes and Barons inclusive as "gentry." To them the gentry are the lesser landowners,
the squires, occupants of good solid houses, often as
ancient and as beautiful as the nobleman's Hall,
but smaller and less lavish in decoration. To the inhabitants of country towns, on the other hand, the
gentry are the professional people — the parsons,
the doctors, the lawyers, the retired officers and
Civil Servants, the masters in Public Schools (if
there are any), and the men or women of modest
"independent means," dependent upon speculation
or the labour of other people which produces their
dividends. Thus the gentry may be rural and urban,
but put together they form a class peculiarly representative of the English. In fact, they are the class

by which we are chiefly judged abroad, now that the age has long passed when every Englishman who crossed the Channel could be addressed as "my Lord."

Even the word "gentry" does not include the whole class, for it is used only in the country and in country towns. No one would speak of the gentry of Harley Street or of the Temple, except in mockery. In our great cities the professional classes have lost the term because they have no land, not even gardens, and are not personally known to their neighbours. One hesitates to call both sections "the educated classes," for some of the aristocracy and some of the upper middle classes also are educated. So perhaps "The Gentry" must stand, though it comes dangerously near the word "gentlemen," which time is rendering obsolete, together with the top-hat which was formerly one of their insignia, and is still considered suitable for funerals, racecourses, and a royal garden-party.

Nowadays the word "Gentlemen" is painted on lavatory doors, and the half-educated call each other gentlemen, where others would use the word "man" or "fellow." Only the vulgar speak of "gents" to distinguish men from women, and the words "genteel" and "gentility" are used only to sneer at Early Victorian elegance. One feels a fear of the decline already threatening in Tennyson's praise of his departed friend:

"And thus he bore without abuse
    The grand old name of gentleman,
    Defamed by every charlatan,
And soil'd with all ignoble use." [1]

Charlatans have defamed it now, and ignoble use
has soiled it, but pleasant associations still hang
round the word, and, like a ruined abbey, it retains
an antiquarian charm, though no longer consecrated to public worship.

Our working classes also maintain some shadow
of the original meaning when, as a mark of deepest
disapproval, they cry, "You're no gentleman!" or
"Call yourself a gentleman?" before engaging in
active conflict, and a good many elaborate definitions of the old-fashioned word have been attempted. In his admirable book on "England"
Dean Inge quotes various examples from great authorities, such as Dean Church, Cardinal Newman,
Ruskin, Lowell, and Professor Santayana. A few
sentences may be extracted. Dean Church, writing
of the *Faerie Queen*, traced the slow growth of the
English gentleman as gradually gaining something
beyond noble blood and family honours:

"The idea of manhood," he writes, "was to grow into
that high type of cultivated English nature, in the nineteenth and the eighteenth centuries, common both to its
monarchical and its democratic embodiments, than which,
with all its faults and defects, our western civilization has
produced few things more admirable."

[1] *In Memoriam:* cxi (1850).

And Cardinal Newman begins his description
with the words : " It is almost a definition of the gentleman to say that he is one who never inflicts pain."
I have seen that definition expanded into "One who
never unintentionally inflicts pain," which opens the
door to all manner of cynical reservations, and
would exclude nearly all sportsmen and the whole
profession of our flogging schoolmasters. But the
Cardinal continues :

> "The true gentleman never speaks of himself except
> when compelled, never defends himself by a mere retort,
> he has no ears for slander or gossip, is scrupulous in im-
> puting motives to those who interfere with him, and in-
> terprets everything for the best. He has too much sense
> to be affronted at insult, he is too busy to remember in-
> juries, and too indolent to bear malice. Nowhere shall we
> find greater candour, conciliation, indulgence." [1]

Let me add one more national description, and
the estimate of two distinguished foreigners. Writing in 1872, Taine, in his familiar *Notes on England*,
wrote :

> "Dr. Arnold, when travelling in France, wrote to his
> friends, 'What strikes me here is the total absence of
> gentlemen, and of all persons having the education and the
> sentiments of a real gentleman. There are very few per-
> sons here who have the appearance and manners of one.
> A real English Christian gentleman, of manly heart, en-
> lightened mind, is more, I think, than Guizot or Sismondi
> could be able to comprehend; no other country could, I
> think, furnish so fine a specimen of human nature.' Strip

[1] Quotations from Dean Inge's *England*, p. 58 ff.

off these exaggerations of national self-love, instructive
testimony will remain. For them, a real gentleman is a
real noble, a man worthy of commanding, upright, disin-
terested, capable of exposing himself and even of sacri-
ficing himself for those whom he leads, not only an honourable man, but a conscientious man in whom generous
instincts have been confirmed by straightforward reflection, and who, acting naturally well, acts still better upon
principle. In this ideal portrait, you recognize the accomplished chief; add to it the English varieties, empire over
self, continuous coolness, perseverance in adversity, natural seriousness, dignity of manner, the shunning of all
affectation or boasting . . ." [1]

And so on, in flattering terms that Mr. Podsnap
might have adopted. In partial contrast, take a
recent German estimate. Writing of our Public
Schools, Professor Dibelius observes:

"Here is trained the dyed-in-the-wool Conservative
gentleman, who has never heard of Ibsen, who crosses
himself at the mention of Bolshevism, who thinks, as his
newspaper tells him from time to time, that Lloyd George
is either the greatest of Englishmen or the scum of humanity, who treats women with unfailing tact and politeness, who resents any infraction of his own sense of right
and who, in some remote Indian court, will rule millions
without any external power, simply by his skill and energy
as Resident. It is a type that everywhere rules men and
knows them; despising any sort of problem as mere moon-
shine, and compels even the unwilling outsider to recog-
nise its great effective efficiency." [2]

[1] Taine's *Notes on England*, p. 174; translated by W. F. Rae (1872).
[2] *England*, by Professor Dibelius, p. 466, translated by Mary Agnes
Hamilton (1930).

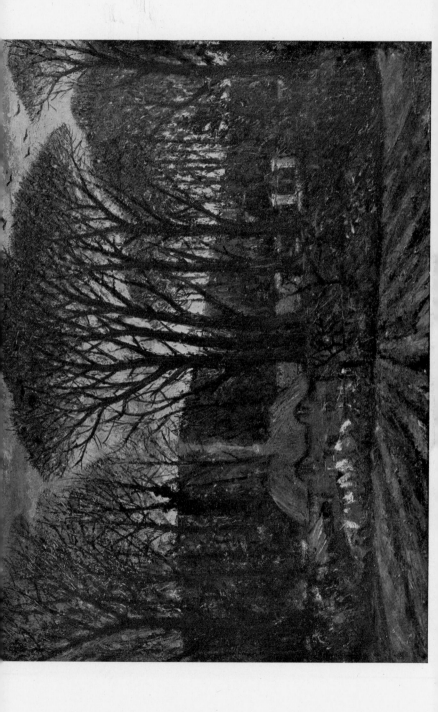

To turn from generalities to a particular instance: Professor Gilbert Murray, in one of his recent books, draws a picture of a man who, I cannot doubt, was his father:

"Seventy years ago," he writes, "a traveller in the Australian bush, riding up at nightfall to a solitary wooden cabin in the district between the Murray and Murrumbidgee rivers, would have found the owner sitting alone at a rough and frugal dinner, in complete evening dress. He wore evening dress for the sake of its associations, because he and his people had done so at home. It was to him part of a tradition of thought and conduct and social atmosphere which he valued and which he felt himself to be in danger of losing. He wore it with emphasis and deliberately, though it was, in his present circumstances, a habit both unusual and inconvenient.

"To the man in evening dress the tradition represented an ideal. The tradition expected him to be an educated man and a gentleman, to keep his word, to control his desires and passions, and as a part and parcel of the same attitude, to sit down as clean at his meals in the remote bush as he would in his father's house. The tradition represented a memory which he loved and was proud of, and to which he intended to be true."[1]

I have found that man all over the world, dressed just like Gilbert Murray's instance, except that in Nigeria a soft shirt and collar are ordained, because the damp heat and sweat reduce starched things to pulp in half an hour.

Those definitions or descriptions are mostly very

[1] *The Classical Tradition in Poetry*, by Gilbert Murray, pp. 3 and 5 (1927).

pretty and partly true. But here comes "furious Ruskin and sticks his tusk in" (a rhyme he rather enjoyed) with his grim warning:

> "Gentlemen will have to learn, that it is no part of their duty or privilege to live on others' toil. They have to learn that there is no degradation in the hardest manual labour or the most servile labour while it is honest. But there is degradation, and that deep, in extravagance, in bribery, in indolence, in pride, in taking places they are not fit for, or in coining places for which there is no need."

"That's hard," as the exquisite Millamant says in *The Way of the World*. It would have been incomprehensible to the gentry of the eighteenth century, when the truest types of this class were to be found — the types that were so innocently pictured by Reynolds, Gainsborough, and Zoffany; perhaps not quite innocently by Hogarth. In those pictures we see them still — the debonair gentlemen, ruddy and substantial, with their hounds and long-nosed, thin-necked horses, their long coats, yellow waistcoats, and fine grey breeches; the long-faced, long-nosed, long-lipped women, so demure, so dull, so secure in their tight laces and ample skirts of gleaming satin. Others again, consciously elegant and *dilettanti* as Horace Walpole, taking the air in a park or discoursing music in a boudoir. There we see the English gentry in their finest bloom, and if furious Ruskin had stuck his tusk in, telling them it was no part of their duty or their privilege to live on others' toil, they would have turned their keepers on to him as a wild boar. They were the squires, the gentry, the upper classes. They were unquestionably satisfied with the position, and had no doubt of their right to it. They were the parents of Jane Austen's delightful people, who still had no doubts, and would have regarded manual labour as a degradation too deep for thought, an unimaginable interruption to their dances, passionless flirtations, sauntering teas, medicinal waters, colds, and gruel.[1]

" Independent means ! " You may still hear working people and country labourers say that so-and-so is "a gentleman," meaning that he does not work for his living. They will even say that a working tradesman has been "made a gentleman of" by inheriting a large sum of money, just as they say a man makes his mistress an honest woman by marrying her. There is still a tendency to draw the line of gentility according to income, the employment of more than one domestic servant, and if one of them is male, so much the better. The independent means derived from rents or dividends must be sufficient to pay servants to do the housework and gardening, or else the livelihood must be derived from the Church, the law, medicine, the army or navy, the stock-exchange (rather dubious), art (more dubious), or literature (hardly to be considered).

In country districts, the gentry are reckoned, even by the aristocrats, as belonging to "The County,"

[1] The "Conversation Pictures" exhibited in Sir Philip Sassoon's house (25 Park Lane) in March, 1930, revealed the type of gentry above described.

and unless they have lost money by speculation, taxation, or attempts to farm their own land, their homes are arranged on the best model of solid English comfort—a word which foreigners have been obliged to borrow, just as we have borrowed the word *finesse* because we have none. In estimating conditions to which so many English people have been accustomed all their lives, it is useful to take the opinion of clever and observant foreigners, as, for instance, the Czech, Karel Čapek, who thus describes life in an English country house:

> "Tennis and warm water, the gong summoning you to lunch, books, meadows, comfort selected, stabilized, and blest by the centuries, freedom of children and patriarchal disposition of parents, hospitality and a formalism as comfortable as a dressing-gown."

And later on, speaking of the elder inhabitants of these comfortable homes, Čapek writes:

> "The most beautiful things in England are the trees, the herds, and the people; and then, too, the ships. But old England comprises those rosy old gentlemen who in the spring-time wear grey top-hats, and in the summer chase tiny balls over golf-courses, and they look so fresh and nice that I should like to play with them if I were eight years old; and the old ladies who always have some knitting in their hands and are rosy, nice-looking and kind, drink hot water and never tell you about their ailments." [1]

That is excellent, but there is a stronger quality beneath all that sweetness and jollity. An English-

[1] *Letters from England*, by Karel Čapek, pp. 83 and 170.

woman, who was herself born and brought up in one of those country houses, tells of other duties besides golf and knitting. She writes:

"A sense of responsibility for the village and country-side was the dominating factor in the ordering of country-house life. The whole family lived on a pedestal. The land-lord must set an example. Tenants, employés, household servants, all took their cue from him. His actions were matters of real importance, his influence paramount. It mattered intensely if he went to church or not, if he sub-scribed to one local charity rather than another; if he patronized the hunt ball, the flower-show, the cricket-match; if his wife called on Mrs. So-and-so. All village institutions originated in the Hall. The landlord's county work obliged him to live in the light of publicity. . . . The Hall provided all the culture and all the recreation for the village at its door; all the material assistance of dis-tress too, for in periods of sickness or trouble it was the lady at the Hall who supplemented incredible wages by puddings and beef-tea, by blankets and flannel petticoats. . . . 'The poor' were a race apart, different in all essen-tials, both physical and spiritual to the rich. 'I do love the poor'; such and such a thing would be 'bad for the poor' — such familiar expressions revealed the gulf." [1]

Nowadays one would gasp at hearing anyone talk about "the poor," but it is not so long ago since I was brought up to think they had a divinely ordained and unalterable position in the world, and Hannah More, who died in 1833, piously be-lieved they were put here by the Almighty to give

[1] *Old and New in the Countryside*, by Victoria de Bunsen (born Buxton), pp. 12, 13 (1920).

the rich so many opportunities for the virtue of charity.

Where the Halls, manors, or country houses of the type described still survive, they are pervaded by a recognizable, clean smell, derived from fragrant spices in the store-room, and from generations of furniture-polish applied to the oaken tables and the wainscoting on the walls. The walls themselves are often adorned with the grandfather's curving sword, and with coloured prints representing British soldiers in red coats and amazing head-dresses, charging hordes of Hindus, Russians, or the French Old Guard at Waterloo. And they may represent a man-of-war in full sail, or the engagement between the *Shannon* and the *Chesapeake*. The tradition of war as the noblest of all occupations is thus early inculcated upon the children, and it was from this class that the best officers in the navy and the regular army were chiefly drawn before the Great War.

Other pictures in the dining-room remind the family of favourite horses and dogs, or of hunting scenes upon the undulating fields of the Shires. In the stone-flagged entrance hall a few stuffed heads of antlered stags look down with glassy eyes to greet the visitor, and in glass cases all around the walls may be seen stuffed trout, salmon, or pike of unusual dimensions, their weight and the place and date of their deaths being carefully recorded on labels, as on tombstones without scriptural texts.

The debonair inheritors of these houses often contrive to scrape together money enough to send at least one son into the army or navy; if possible into the regiment or arm of service in which his forefathers have served. Other sons are sent, if means allow, to one of the famous Public Schools, often connected with the family for generations. And at least one will complete his education at a University, especially if there is a Family Living in the gift of the father or a considerate relation. But learning is seldom pursued with a hunter's zest, even by the candidate for Holy Orders, and to pass into a University or the army many Public School boys are obliged to seek a sufficiency of knowledge at a crammer's. I am told things are changed since my time at an ancient Public School, where learning was naturally despised, and a boy who worked hard to excel in it lost caste almost as much as if he stole, or lied to anyone but a master, who was "fair game."

In that fine old school, learning was not of the kind to capture the attention of the average English boy. No natural science of any kind was taught, and mathematics were regarded as an inexplicable joke. The only study thought worthy of us was Greek, with Latin as a subordinate pursuit. In both tongues accuracy of translation and composition was the only aim, and the value of the classical writers in literature or history was hardly considered. When I now visit my old school, removed to a former workhouse upon a plateau across the Severn, I am told of a "Modern Side," where mathematics and science are regularly taught, and on the "Classical Side" the writers of antiquity are illustrated by photographs of Greece and Rome, maps, lectures on their literary and historic worth, and even by dramatic performances. I cannot doubt that the sons of the gentry profit by this remarkable change, and in Oxford I perceive a change even more salutary.

But neither in school nor University have I noticed a change in the adoration devoted to games and the physical prowess displayed in the sports of cricket, football, and the art of propelling slim boats upon rivers. These muscular labours are supposed to keep Englishmen "fit." "Fit for what?" asks the critic in *Punch* (March 1930), and there is no answer to that Socratic questioner. The boy or youth who excels at any game is assured of popularity among his fellows and the respectful approval of masters and dons, though perhaps he does no work, hangs about at the bottom of the school, and cannot pass the University exams. "You may work or not as you like," says the head master in another old *Punch,* as he prepares the flogging. "But play you must and shall!"

It is unusual for a head master to incite to energy in games by these violent means, but among the boys themselves it is customary. In my own school the Upper Sixth did not flog, but they enjoyed the privilege of kicking a boy who shirked football, they standing in rows while he passed down between them, as at a country dance. At an equally famous school, an athlete of high reputation tells that when he was thirteen he went to practise rowing on the river instead of watching the final in a House cricket-match, and for this indifference to the honour of the House the captain gave him eleven blows with a cane which made him black for many weeks and marked him for a year. At the same school, if the House lost at football, each member of the team got five strokes with a cane, to encourage the rest.

But in most Public Schools, perhaps still in all, the head master flogs with birch or cane in the hope of stimulating to industry or better conduct. In my school birching was a recognized and fairly regular pastime, and it was the weekly monitor's duty to attend on the occasion and hold back the victim's shirt. At another great school, all the masters and prefects might flog, and all did. One boy was flogged twenty or thirty times every term, and the head master, equally distinguished for athletics and theology, won the further distinction of repeatedly striking the same place with the cane so as to draw blood through the trousers.

Many boys, now grown into men, wax enthusiastic over their past sufferings, loudly proclaiming that the floggings "made us what we are, by Jove!" as though they assumed they had reached the pinnacle of human perfection. At one school the cost of the birching was entered on the parents' bill as " School medicine "; at another as " Special tuition," and there is a touch of English irony about the terms. But clever and sensitive boys often suffer intensely from the expectation of pain and horror. At one school I have known boys so overwhelmed with horror at the deliberate caning of others in the centre of a circle composed of the whole school, that they fell into profound and cheerless melancholy. To them the performance was a public execution, and they could not endure it.

But the effect upon the master or prefect is still worse. He is supposed to wait until anger or rage is passed, and then, in cold blood, to strike his helpless victim again and again with the chilly and deliberate purpose of inflicting pain. Certainly, there are men who take a sadistic or sensual delight in this foul action, but usually the effect must be the same as that the hanging of a man has upon the executioner. The only possibly good point in this device for producing the English gentleman is that it may accustom the boy, like a Spartan boy, to conceal the emotion of fear, and to silence the expression of pain. The suppression of emotion, especially of fear, is certainly part of the Englishman's character, and a valuable part. But in America, France, or Germany do they retain flogging in the hope of making an American, French, or German gentleman? If not, what substitute do they find? Or do they despair of making a gentleman at all?

Suckled upon the traditions of the country house, and confirmed in the traditions of beautiful Public

Schools and beautiful Universities (both too ener-
vating in beauty for prolonged residence), the English gentleman is packed off to the administration
of an Empire over peoples developed from no such
traditions at all. Yet in far-away lands he may become an excellent official and employer of native
labour. For his intimate acquaintance with horses
and dogs has taught him how to deal with the un-
tutored mind, and, so long as he can say, "Good
dog! Fetch it, then!" he is fairly successful. Trouble
may come if the native population spring from
a stock more akin to our own, but even then the
boy's inbred sense of justice and his honesty about
money will generally avert disaster. Sometimes
also his youthful association with animals has
taught him a sympathetic kindliness; for the Englishman is seldom cruel except to the foxes, deer,
otters, and other animals which he kills for his
pleasure.

Like the sons of a country family, the daughters
learn a good deal about horses, dogs, and motors.
By pottering about the house and gardens they
learn a certain amount of housekeeping, cookery,
and the growth of flowers, fruit, and vegetables.
They enjoy hunting, shooting, dancing, tennis, golf,
ministering to "the poor," and ratting with terriers
and an iron spud. In a recent story of country life,
the heroine whose beauty upset the equanimity of
every male in the neighbourhood, gives the following cheerful account of how she passed her days:

"I dig," Carrie said. "When I'm not district-visiting, or giving Sunday School lessons, or practising some new songs for a concert, or entertaining, I dig in the garden, or weed in the garden, or spud up plantains, or grub up white clover from the tennis-courts. In the winter I hunt about once a fortnight, when my poor mare's legs aren't filled, and in the summer I play tennis, whenever I'm not weeding. I'm like the old horse in Watts's picture — 'A simple life of unregarded toil.'" [1]

The reference to a Watts picture sounds a little old-fashioned, or out of place. But it is quite right, for mixed up among the battle pictures, stuffed stags, fish, and foxes' tails, one can quite imagine photographs of "Hope" and "Love and Death" in the lovely girl's bedroom. Naturally the daughters of the family keep their wits alert for marriage, and their real accomplishments, which now go far beyond deportment, and often include a little music and better French than their future husbands can command, fit them to become wives of the few clergymen who can afford them, Indian and Colonial Civil Servants, army officers, or neighbouring squires. Thus they hand on the English blood and the old tradition. Indeed, the versatility of both sons and daughters is so enviable that, in case of revolution in this country, or of a sudden reversal in the family fortune, they would not be so futile as the charming people in Tchekhov's *Cherry Orchard*, but would probably make their own living just as well as the Russian aristocrats who, having escaped

[1] *The Hawbucks*, by John Masefield, p. 156 (1929).

from the wrath to come, now contrive to live by working as chauffeurs, grooms, waiters, cooks, and restaurant keepers in Constantinople, Berlin, Vienna, Paris, and London.

Upon a large number of the country gentry the reversal of fortune has fallen since the war. These are the "New Poor," and their places are now taken by profiteers, speculators, and others of the "New Rich." It is interesting to enquire how much further advanced in the niceties of civilization the New Rich may be than their immediate predecessors. We may assume it must have been to entice the New Rich into the habits expected of their present position that the two following advertisements appeared in fashionable papers :

"Here (in a certain named sanatorium for dogs) they (the dogs) are strictly dieted. If a tonic is needed, virol or cod-liver oil is given. At eleven o'clock many dogs have raw eggs as a pick-me-up. When a dog is a bit nervy he is given ultra-violet ray treatment. Long week-end motor trips are very tiring and trying, and to speed along in an open car hurts his (dog's) eyes. At (a place named) there are motor-goggles for dogs, tailored overcoats that come well over the chest, nice, soft, serviceable travelling rugs, handkerchiefs to wipe the eyes."

Other similar accessories to modern civilization follow, and in an advertisement of a watering-place in France one reads :

"Whether it be round the green cloth of the gambling rooms or the green golf links or polo ground, one mixes with none but gentlefolk. That is why there is no other place like (name given). Everything there is calm, select, courteous, dignified, and this applies not only to the strollers, among whom one notices many members of the British aristocracy, but also the opalescent tint of the sky, to the mild, soft, joy-giving air, which seems ever to sound with the peal of a perpetual Sunday." [1]

It is instructive to think of those raw eggs and violet rays, those tailored overcoats and handkerchiefs to wipe the eyes. Also to think of those members of the British aristocracy, that opalescent sky, that air which seems to sound with the peal of a perpetual Sunday! Mankind in all his history has never reached such a height of refinement and piety.

And yet, in spite of the solemn warning given the old inhabitants in Bernard Shaw's *Heartbreak House,* it seems a pity that, owing to loss of sons and the taxation for the war, they should be driven out to make room for new-comers who will never know carrots from parsley or rabbits from rats, and will use the ancient buildings as a motor-garage or a scene for week-end dissipation with crooked speculators and greedy concubines. After all, the old squires and their families did give a certain charm to the countryside. They were part of the English fauna, and perhaps the type is now seen at its best just because it is vanishing; even as a mackerel displays its most brilliant colours as it dies, and a crab gleams with phosphorus before it stinks. But per-

[1] Quoted from the original advertisements by "Yaffle" in the *New Leader* of September 30, 1927, and May 25, 1928.

sonally I regret the disappearance of the squire even more than the disappearance of the nobleman, for I should always feel more at home in Heartbreak House than in Horseback Hall.[1]

II. THE PROFESSIONAL CLASSES

Closely connected with the gentlefolk of the country houses is the professional man. He is often sprung from the same stock as the squire, and if he has attained to a substantial position and kept up his sportsmanlike interests, the squire feels no hesitation in associating with him, and may allow a son to marry his daughter without a qualm. The professional man, especially the schoolmaster, is the Englishman best known abroad, because he is an energetic tourist and likes to spend his vacations in scaling precipices, gazing at famous pictures, and photographing ancient towns. Having received the highest education that England can give, he seldom speaks any human language but his own, though a polite waiter will understand his simple-hearted efforts at French. Foreigners know him at once by his enviable clothing, which sets a fashion for Continental males; by the amount he eats at breakfast; by his resolution to have a table to himself, by his demands for *The Times, Punch,* a bath, and marmalade, and by his habit of carrying about a thin piece of wood three feet long. On the whole he is popular, for he makes no fuss, pays his bill without

[1] See the Preface to Bernard Shaw's *Heartbreak House* (1919).

reading it, gives bigger tips than a Frenchman or a German, speaks seldom, and then in quiet and rather pleasing tones, and observes the foreigners' ways with a superior curiosity that never forgets the England in his soul.

The Englishwoman travelling alone is less popular than the Englishman, for she is inclined to be apprehensive of unknown perils, apt to make a fuss about her luggage and bills and tips; nor is she accepted by Continental women as setting the fashion in feminine dress. She asks for tea at unimaginable hours, and though she does not demand marmalade and *The Times* with such persistence as the man, she always keeps her superior character and nationality in mind. "What do you as a foreigner think of our cities?" asked an amiable German of the English lady on a Rhine steamboat. "I'm not a foreigner. I'm English," was the inevitable reply. But, if she is young, she over-smokes to display her emancipation, and burns holes in the chair-covers and carpets with her cigarettes.

So the English gentleman and the English lady go upon their way, indifferent to ridicule because it never occurs to them to think they can be ridiculous; but equally indifferent to Mr. Rudyard Kipling's adulation of their race, and his brag about "The Blood" and its elevatingly close connection with "The Lord." For they have been trained from the cradle never to brag. At home and at school they have been trained never to show emotion; especially, as I noticed above, never to show fear. But also never to show grief or affection in public. Everyone feels fear, but the Englishman must not show it. A large number feel affection, but the Englishman must not show it in public. A mother who kisses her son before his schoolfellows is hardly pardonable, and the boy prefers it to be supposed that he never had any relations, unless indeed his father was a " Blue," and rowed in the 'Varsity Eight or played in the Eleven, or won an "event" in the Sports.

This power of self-control, drilled into the Englishman by example and precept from childhood and called by foreigners the English "phlegm," is one of his three most valuable and characteristic qualities. For it saves him from whining and wailing, from explosions of temper, and from rhetoric. In face of a dangerous crisis he will keep quiet, and he will not pour out lamentations over the irretrievable past. John Stuart Mill thought this restraint tended to kill fine emotions by atrophy. But I think the danger lies the other way. The suppression or constraint of emotion, especially of love for women, may bank it up till it bursts out in glacial flood, or blazes like the eruption of a volcano long supposed to be extinct.

The second admirable quality of our gentry and professional class is the refusal to take bribes. Perhaps "refusal" is too strong a word, for he would be a daring man who even attempted to bribe this type of gentleman. "It would be like violating a nun!" as a "crook" once said to me, when for a moment he contemplated buying a private advantage from an English official. It is seldom thought of, and it is hardly ever done. Our Civil Servants in India, for instance, have repeated opportunities of making a lot of money by taking bribes, but I remember only one case of even a suspicion of corruption. This reputation for incorruptibility is the greatest of our advantages in administering the Empire. Its rarity among nearly all the other peoples I have known raises our officials almost to the level of divine superiority, and without it we could not hold the Empire together, nor would it be worth the pains. A business man who has worked long under the system of concessions in Russia tells me that it is now impossible to bribe the Commissars or other high officials there. That is an immense advance, for under the Tsarism one had only to signify the chance of a good bribe and one got what was wanted. But nowadays on the suspicion of bribery both parties are shot offhand. It is a drastic way of teaching what we have somehow learnt so smoothly that we are scarcely conscious of the lesson or of our need of it. Yet there was need. Less than two centuries ago, bribery ran riot among our aristocracy and politicians, so that a Prime Minister could boast that every man had his price. The change is remarkable, and in spite of all that can be justly said against our Public Schools, I think it may be traced to an unconscious sense of honour somehow instilled among the boys. In my school I remember only one case of theft, and though in a still more famous school I was lately told that the boys constantly " pinch " each other's possessions, I should like to attribute that habit to the growth of a fraternal communism among them. " Friends' things are common property," as Aristotle said in three words (Κοινὰ τῶν φίλων).

Equally valuable in our dealings with natives and other foreigners is the English gentleman's reputation for keeping his word. For instance, in walking through rarely visited parts of Central Africa, I found it sufficient to tell my carriers that I would give them each so many yards of cloth (calico) per week or per month. Simply because I was an Englishman they took my word without hesitation or further agreement, and tramped along through deserts and forests, carrying my baggage on their heads together with the bales of cloth which were to be their reward. When at the end I measured out the proper lengths from finger-tip to finger-tip of my outstretched arms and sent them all away happy, I felt grateful to any Englishman who might have travelled that way, from Livingstone downwards. I remembered how Livingstone, after reaching the coast at Loanda and standing within a few weeks' journey of England and fame, quietly turned back into the centre of unknown Africa again so as not to break faith with the Barotze men who did not

dare return to their country without him.[1] " He
that sweareth to his neighbour and disappointeth
him not, though it be to his own hurt," is a good
Hebrew suggestion of this excellent quality, owing
to which the Englishman's word is still accepted as
his bond in many distant countries. And, personally, I have always found the Jews following their
own estimation of the man who may dwell in the
Lord's holy hill, though their bond may be strictly
enforced.[2]

The English gentleman's third most valuable and
characteristic quality is his instinct for " Fair Play."
The phrase arose from his habits in sport and games.
Even if he wishes very much to kill a beast, bird, or
fish, he will give it a " sporting chance " of life. He
will not shoot a bird sitting, unless he is very raven-
ous, or blow out a wild beast's brains at close range,
unless he is in great danger. He will not net trout
or grouse or pheasants, nor will he join in the rabbit
coursing that allows the rabbit no way of escape.
That would not be fair play. Neither is it fair play
to win a game by a trick or by a breach of the rules.
Again, the English do not think it fair play to un-
nerve and baffle an opponent's team at football by
raising yells of derision and shrieks of spiteful con-
tumely against them, though it is allowable to cheer
one's own side. In the United States, among the

[1] It was in 1854 at the end of his great exploration from Cape Colony
north-west. See his *Missionary Travels in South Africa*, Chap. XX.

[2] See Psalm xv, 5. I have combined the Prayer Book translation with
the Authorized Version.

spectators at a baseball match, the custom is different, perhaps owing to the reported exciting superiority of the American atmosphere.

This instinct of fair play has extended throughout the daily life of these Upper Classes, until it has become a rule of conduct. To describe a man as " fair game " implies that he is a fool or a knave, a fit object to be caricatured, insulted, derided, or even assaulted without breach of propriety. But to say that some action "isn't cricket " implies moral and social condemnation. When, for instance, a girl upon a liner had just become engaged to one passenger, and was then approached with passionate insistence by another, she protested, " No! I'm sorry, but to kiss you wouldn't be cricket!" The phrase might have puzzled a French lover, but it sufficed.

Akin to this instinct of fair play are the unwritten rules of "Good Form." Like fair play, these rules have been gradually and unconsciously evolved at the Public Schools and Universities to which the Upper Class of the English people chiefly resort, if parents can afford the expense. Unhappily for the rest of our population, numbering about 97 per cent, the expense is beyond their means. To enjoy the complete education of the English gentleman, a boy should be sent at the age of eight, nine or ten to a Preparatory School, where he will receive education for about four years at the rate of about £200 a year. He will then proceed to a Public School, where his education will be continued for four or five years at the rate of £250 or £300 a year. He will then proceed to Oxford or Cambridge, where his education will be completed in three or more, probably four, years at the rate of £250, £300, or £400 a year. The amount spent upon the education of one single boy, therefore, comes to about £3000, and on an average the amount spent upon this advantage during the years, let us say, from ten to twenty-two would be equal year by year to the wages a well-paid workman would get to support himself and his family in housing, food, and clothes. The amount spent upon the education of an English lady is less, but not much less. So that it is obviously beyond the means of the great majority of the English people ever to become gentlemen and ladies, and so to obtain a perfect knowledge of " Good Form."

This is unfortunate, for a sin against the rules of Good Form, though not criminal in the eyes of the law, is more disgraceful than crime. Among the comparatively small but important class referred to, those rules have, in fact, superseded the Ten Commandments, and are far more strictly observed, at all events than the Fourth and Seventh. For instance, under the section of Dress Commandments, which are the simplest and most easily acquired, may be counted the prescribed rules: (1) Thou shalt not wear a black tie with a long evening coat; and its converse, Thou shalt not wear a white tie with a short evening coat; (2) Thou shalt not

have less than four buttons on a dress waistcoat;
(3) Thou shalt not tuck the corners of thy white ties
under the points of thy dress collar; (4) Thou shalt
not wear brown boots or light socks with dark
trousers; (5) Thou shalt not wear a low hat with
a long black coat, nor a tall hat with a short coat of
any colour; (6) Thou shalt not display a coloured
handkerchief with evening dress. Unlike the Ten
Commandments, the rules of Good Form differ for
the two sexes, at all events in the Dress Department.

Such commandments may appear trivial to people
accustomed to a sterner code dealing with murder,
embezzlement, and theft. But the penalties attach-
ing to a breach of them are not trivial. I have known
a man ostracized among the first-class passengers in
a liner because he broke the Commandment against
wearing a black tie with a long dress-coat. He erred
in ignorance, but, as in English law, ignorance is no
excuse. Like the British Constitution, or like those
eternal and heaven-born laws to which Antigone
appealed, the Commandments of Good Form are
unwritten, and can be learnt only by association
with the class in which they are binding. It is no
good praying to that class to incline your heart to
keep this law, if you do not know what the law is,
and at any moment a member of the 97 per cent
among our population may offend unconsciously.
I have sometimes thought the position of the tens of
millions among our fellow-subjects in this country
who are hopelessly excluded for ever from a sphere

of knowledge so vital is rather hard. For at the very best, an innocent offender against the rules of Good Form can never rise higher than to be called a " nature's gentleman," and I cannot imagine a more painful commendation.

On these three attributes of self-control, honesty, and fair play, is founded that finest type of the " English gentleman," accepted upon the Continent with respectful amusement. For he is well-dressed, pays his bill, is clean in his habits, avoids his own countrymen, and never speaks to a foreigner. The type is a product of family tradition carried forward by the Public School, the old Universities, and the training colleges for naval and military officers. It produces the great majority of the Anglican clergy (though the demand in the Church now exceeds the supply), the masters in the Public Schools (so that the tradition is perpetuated), nearly all barristers, most solicitors, some doctors, and a few journalists, though the education is rightly regarded as a disqualification for the kind of journalism established by Lord Northcliffe at the end of last century. Men of the same University or the same School hang together most closely with natural, unreasonable fidelity, but among all men of this type one feels an instinctive friendliness — a kind of Freemasonry — springing partly from similar habits and behaviour, but chiefly from a justified assumption that one member of the class will not swindle or " jockey " another, just as dog will not eat dog. The bond is even stronger, for dog will eat dog under Arctic conditions, but both within the Arctic Circle and upon the Equator I have felt safe from being devoured by men of this type.

It has sometimes happened that members of the Episcopal and Ministerial Benches have appeared to owe their high position chiefly to their recorded prowess on the river or the cricket-field or at football and the running track. But as a rule it is the scholars who take the lead in professions such as the Church, the Bar, and Politics, in which corporeal agility plays but a secondary part. By a careful inspection of Ministerial records, Professor Harold Laski has shown that the great majority of the Parliamentary Ministers have been educated at the Public Schools and Universities. Some of these, like Mr. Gladstone, Mr. Asquith, Lord Milner, and Lord Curzon, have been distinguished Oxford scholars, and nearly all of them have imbibed the modicum of learning provided in those institutions for all who can afford it.

But commendable as our scholar statesmen have sometimes proved themselves, I think the country owes most to this professional class for its supply of Civil Servants and officers in the navy and army. I suppose that our regimental officers are the best in the world, and their excellence is due to a high tradition and the habit of team-work in the Schools. It is true that the routine of those traditions and habits may stifle the intuitive genius that makes the

finest generals, but we are a nation of captains. My
own experience of the navy has not been so intimate, but I have seen a good deal of naval officers
on manœuvres and during the Dardanelles campaign, and have recognized in them the qualities of
the class. As for the Civil Servants whom this class
supplies both for home and for India, praise can
hardly be too high.

Let us omit India, as the Empire is too vast for
the limits of this brief treatise, though what I have
seen of the Civil Servants in India fills me with admiration for their silent devotion, courage, and up-
rightness. But here in England we have a set of
educated and clever men who might have earned
distinction and possibly wealth in any other profession. It is true that many may have chosen the
Service for its immediate income and its security.
But there they are, content to sink their individu-
ality and ambition in the service of the State, to remain entirely unknown outside their own offices,
to labour year after year at routine work, usually
dull and monotonous, and all for an income that
will rise but slowly to a moderate competence, ending in a retiring pension and oblivion, when their
contemporaries in other lines of work have just
reached the height of fame and fortune. Certainly
one of them long ago said to me, " Your future is
very uncertain, but as a Civil Servant I shall be ten
pounds happier every year." Yet many of them toil
with real devotion for their branch. It is seldom that

a charge of corruption can be even whispered against them, and they have served every Government, even a Labour Government, with equal loyalty, in spite of one or two reputed exceptions.

I used to regard Socialism with suspicion because, if the State controlled all wealth and production, the powers of the bureaucracy must be enormously increased, and the bureaucrat seemed likely to become the slave of his machine, to work as little as he could with decency, and sulkily to oppose any change likely to involve more trouble. But the example of many Civil Servants whom I have known now makes me hopeful that these natural fears were exaggerated. In the silent hours of his obscurity a Civil Servant will work simply because he likes to do the work well, and if he sees public advantage in a change he will even struggle to adapt his private convenience to it rather than comfortably to obstruct. One might say that the excellence of the English Civil Service is the strongest argument that Socialists could use.

Another marked characteristic of the "gentleman" is an imaginative sympathy, sometimes shown as tact, sometimes as charm, or merely as helpfulness. Tact and charm are generally accounted feminine attributes, but I have known men who possessed them. Such, for instance, was the late Lord Pentland, early known to me as Captain John Sinclair of the 5th Lancers, not a particularly clever man, but possessing the ingrained quality of charm.

There was an old comic song with refrain: " It isn't what he says, but the nasty way he says it." So of Lord Pentland, at one time Governor of Madras, one could say: " It wasn't what he said, but the charming way he said it." Lord Balfour, who died in March, 1930, possessed the same enviable quality, and to such a high degree that it was supposed to imply weakness. Which accounts for his profound self-criticism: " No man ever had charm without being the worse for it."

As for mere helpfulness, let me again quote from the acute and humorous Bohemian observer:

> " A gentleman, that is a measured combination of si-
> lence, courtesy, dignity, sport, newspapers, and honesty.
> The man sitting opposite you in the train will anger you
> for two hours by not regarding you as worthy of a glance;
> suddenly he gets up and hands you your bag which you
> are unable to reach. Here the people always manage to
> help each other, but they never have anything to say to
> each other, except about the weather. That is probably
> why Englishmen have invented all games, and why they
> do not speak during their games." [1]

This spirit of helpfulness is shown in the amazing number of charitable societies and institutions in England, freely supported and often conducted by members of this educated class. When I was paid secretary to a society for supplying working-men's clubs with playing-fields, I was astonished to find myself surrounded upon dreary committees by busy

[1] *Letters from England*, by Karel Čapek, p. 172.

and well-to-do men who had in their time won pleasure and glory upon the cricket-field (the giant W. G. Grace was often among them, always silent), and who were now anxious that working men should have similar opportunities. They came in the spirit of helpfulness; modestly, without display, or hope of reward. It is the same spirit that prompts English men and women of this class to sit on committees, Boards of Guardians (now obsolete), County Councils, hospitals, Settlements, or working people's clubs, to say nothing of extending amusement and even education by entertainments and lectures. By willingly undertaking these unattractive duties they relieve the State of much labour and expense that in other countries fall upon officials and the public taxes.

By such actions the well-to-do class has done much to justify its existence and comfortable condition. Nothing in our country fills me with more amazement than the amount of voluntary work thus accomplished. It is not true that our gentlefolk undertake all this toil as a ransom for their own well-being and security. Such a purpose never enters their minds, any more than it entered the minds of the leaders in the difficult movement for the Emancipation of the Slaves (1833), which was one of the chief blessings ever conferred upon the world by England. And a further proof of this is that they extend the spirit of helpfulness to distant peoples from whom they can expect no danger or interference. With

unselfish goodwill, they contribute large sums for the
conversion of " the heathen " to Anglican and other
forms of Christianity, and when I returned from
witnessing the atrocious persecution of subject races
by the Turks early in this century, I had no difficulty in raising enough money to save tens of
thousands from starvation and misery, simply by
narrating what I had seen. Not all contributors belonged to the class we are considering, but the majority did, and I doubt if I could have raised the
same amount from any other European nation.
This was all the more remarkable as the gentry and
professional classes in this country had inherited a
strong bias in favour of the Turks as " the gentlemen of the Near East," and therefore distantly re-
lated to themselves.

CHAPTER VI

THE MIDDLE CLASSES

"Is it not lawful for me to do what I will with mine own?"
St. Matthew xx, 15.

I. THE UPPER MIDDLE

THE CENSUS places only 2.3 per cent of our population above the Middle Classes, and the gulf between the Upper and the Middle was at one time almost impassable. It is still wide, for it is dug on the one side by tradition, and a certain pride in the education which evolves "Good Form"; and on the other side by a pride in dealing with materials called realities, and pecuniary acquisitions called wealth. Both sides of the gulf are trained to express contempt for the other; the Upper Classes regarding the Middle as "banausic" or money-grubbing, the Middle Classes regarding the Upper as foppish and futile. But, in spite of contempt, many on the one side would like to share the wealth of the other, and many on the other side like to rank as "gentlemen," and to have their letters addressed as "Esquire," as though to claim a subservient relationship with the knighthood of chivalry.

The Middle Classes, like the Upper, fall naturally

into two divisions, and the dividing line is here more
distinct than in the former case. The Upper Middle
are distinguished from the Professionals by being
wealthier and less educated (I use "educated" in
the purely English or traditional sense) ; the Lower
Middle are distinguished from the Upper Middle
by being less wealthy but equally uneducated. The
difference of wealth marks the distinction very
clearly as shown by the separate kinds of housing, servants, food, and amusements in the two
classes.

Until well within living memory — say fifty or
sixty years before 1930 — the Upper Middle Class
was extolled as "the backbone of England," much
as in Tudor times agriculture was called "the
paunch of the Commonwealth." It was the steady
and upright support of the whole fabric — a fabric
at that time only recently converted from agriculture to manufacture. John Bright, who was himself
its finest product, was never tired of applauding its
virtues, and recording his own contribution to the
supply of its cheap labour. Mr. Miall, another leader
of the class, maintained that "it had astonished the
world by its energy, enterprise, and self-reliance,
continually striking out new paths of industry, and
subduing the forces of nature." The *Daily News*,
which, with brief intervals, has always striven to
represent this class, in its early days told its readers
that "all the world knew that the great Middle
Class of this country supplies the mind, the will and

the power for all the great and good things that
have been done."[1]

It was as a member of this class in its best days
that Mr. Podsnap addressed to a foreigner the following patriotic remarks:

> "We Englishmen are Very Proud of our Constitution,
> Sir. It was Bestowed upon Us by Providence. No other
> Country is so favoured as This Country. . . .
>
> "This Island was blest, Sir, to the Direct Exclusion of
> such other Countries as — as there may happen to be. And
> if we were all Englishmen present, I would say that there
> is in the Englishman a combination of qualities, a mod-
> esty, and independence, a responsibility, a repose, com-
> bined with an absence of everything calculated to call a
> blush into the cheek of a young person, which one would
> seek in vain among the Nations of the Earth."[2]

And to the man of meek demeanour he asserted,
"There is not a Country in the World, Sir, where so
noble a Provision is made for the poor as in this
Country." Dickens, who well knew the appalling
conditions from which the working classes were just
beginning to emerge, called this phase of the Middle
Class mind " Podsnappery." Matthew Arnold called
the Middle Class outlook upon life " Philistinism,"
the Philistine being, by Schopenhauer's definition, a
man without intellectual needs. The German student means by the word pretty much what the
Frenchman means by *bourgeois*. I quote two of the
passages in which Matthew Arnold condemned

---

[1] Quoted by Matthew Arnold in his essay on *My Countrymen* (1866).
[2] *Our Mutual Friend*, Chapter XI (1865).

the wealthy Middle Class of his day. In one he
makes Culture protest:

> "Consider these people, then, their way of life, their
> habits, their manners, the very tones of their voice; look
> at them attentively; observe the literature they read, the
> things which give them pleasure, the words which come
> forth out of their mouths, the thoughts which make the
> furniture of their minds; would any amount of wealth be
> worth having with the condition that one was to become
> just like these people by having it?"[1]

And he imagines a foreigner saying to him:

> "Drugged with business, your middle class seems to
> have its sense blunted for any stimulus besides, except re-
> ligion; it has a religion, narrow, unintelligent, repulsive.
> . . . What other enjoyments have they? The newspapers,
> a sort of eating and drinking which are not to our taste,
> a literature of books almost entirely religious or semi-
> religious, books utterly unreadable by any educated class
> anywhere, but which your middle class consumes, they
> say, by the hundred thousand; and in their evenings for a
> great treat, a lecture on teetotalism or nunneries. Can any
> life be imagined more hideous, more dismal, more unen-
> viable?"[2]

When those lines were written, the contest seemed
hardly to avail. Those flashing attacks in the name
of "Culture" and "Sweetness and Light" were
aimed against the Upper Middle Classes just at the
height of their power. It is true that Carlyle had
gone before, striking his tremendous blows in *Past*

[1] *Culture and Anarchy: Sweetness and Light* (1869).
[2] *My Countrymen.*

and Present, and the *Latter Day Pamphlets.* Dickens had gone before with *Hard Times,* Ruskin with *Unto this Last,* and Cardinal Newman with his denunciations of "Liberalism." Those in words; Lord Shaftesbury with his Factory Acts in deeds (1844). But the Upper Middle Class still dominated the country, and were the chief leaders in the vast change that befell the countryside and the English people in the first three-quarters of last century. Under their guidance prosperity and population increased beyond the calculation of Malthusians. Mill-owners and mine-owners created a desolation and called it wealth. The midland and northern counties became so thickly veiled in smoke that to this day the sunshine there glimmers, pallid as a ghost. The manufacturing towns spread out into street after street of little brick houses, hideous in monotony, and soon to be blackened by the corrupted air. The clear-flowing rivers were converted, as the North still knows, into black and stinking serpents of poisonous sewage and dye. England was hailed by her own affluent sons as "the workshop of the world," and the Upper Middle Classes flaunted in money, Podsnappery, and Philistinism.

Podsnap, Gradgrind (in *Hard Times*), and Plugson of Undershot (in *Past and Present*) have passed their prime. They have passed, duly belauded by Liberal statesmen for their patriotic service in quadrupling wealth and human hands. Survivals, it is true, may still be recognized, especially in the northern manufacturing regions — men of high living and low thinking, swollen with gross food, motoring, and mental lethargy, until, as I lately watched them wallowing in a salubrious bath at a northern watering-place, I was reminded of the pachyderms' pool at the Zoo. But the shafts of ridicule, the strength of trade-unions, and economic rivalry in Germany, France, India, and Japan have shaken the prestige and self-satisfaction of the class, and its most painful attributes have disappeared or are being mitigated. Some, throwing prudence to the winds, send their sons to the Public Schools and Universities, not so much for the sake of acquiring knowledge as with the more hopeful intention of transforming them into "gentlemen." The seven younger Universities, chiefly in the industrial north, diffuse a mental stimulus, and the art of living is more widely cultivated. I doubt if it would be possible now to find such braggart display of wealth or such insolent contempt for the poverty of professional people as was common in manufacturing cities when I was young. In one ancient but rapidly developing town I knew a monstrous pachyderm, fattened upon the labour of others in his mines and foundries, who boasted that his vulgar habitation was not to be called a house but a Hall, and at a dinner party cried across the table to a refined parson, "Have some more salmon, Mr. Tyrrell! You poor curates don't get salmon every day!"

The pioneers of English industry may all have

been Philistines, but not all were vulgar, and now
that they are disappearing in the due course of mortality we may speak of any fine qualities that we
may remember in them with the spirit of forgiving
epitaphs. They often worked themselves up from
common poverty by steady application, invention,
or ingenuity. They often took a personal interest in
their factories or mines, and stood as patriarchs to
their " hands." I have known workpeople in Yorkshire mills who regarded " the Master " with respect
and affection as a kind of Providence, and with sympathetic consideration, if things were going badly.
For instance when broadcloth for evening dress suddenly went out of fashion, I knew a workman who
said pityingly to the mill-owner, " Never you mind,
Master Willie. Folks gets singing a pack of new-
fangled hymns, but they always come back to the
Old Hundredth. Same with broadcloth, you'll see! "
Broadcloth never has come back, but the mill went
cheerfully on.

This class of wealthy manufacturers, and big or-
ganizers of industry, has been the common butt of
our wits and intellectual professionals for a century
past, and if you shoot at a hippo within easy range
you are likely to hit him somewhere. Being pachy-
dermous he may not feel the wound, even if the
bullet penetrates. But supposing he did feel it and
turned, what might even Plugson of Undershot say?
He probably thinks, and if he could speak at all, he
would say: "What have you foppish, flimsy, and

futile intellectual people, you scornful followers of culture accomplished in England to compare with what I have accomplished? Look at my railways, my ships, my bridges, my tons of unyielding iron and steel, my thousand miles of cotton and cloth, my artificial silk for your daughters' stockings, my sewing machines and thread to stitch your own precious shirts! What can you show to compare? A few thousand books produced every year, each to die within six months at latest, and nearly all of them dealing with imaginary complexities in the procreation of children which I and my kind have always accomplished without any fuss, and to a far greater extent than you seem to be capable of. If you seek a monument to your so-called 'works,' look around at your libraries, sepulchral monuments of your so-called labours, mouldering for ever, untouched, unread. My roads, my railroads, my factories and mines will not live to eternity but they will outlast a hundred generations of your books, your pictures and your pretty fashions.

"If your lives were all a smiling ecstasy like a long summer's day, there might be something to be said for you. But whenever I have the misfortune of meeting one of you, what do I find? Especially among your writers and artists, who make such game of me, it is ten to one I find a pack of irritable, jealous, self-centred people, as unattractive in manner and appearance as I am myself, and dyspeptic besides:

> 'More peevish, cross, and splenetic
> Than dog distract or monkey sick.'

It is as one of your few human-hearted writers has said: ' The philosopher is more frightened and more incompetent in a " real " emergency than the ordinary man : in family life he is more irritable and exhibits less self-control than other men, is just as particular about his food and other " creature comforts." ' [1]

" I thank heaven that my own line of genuine work has protected me from that kind of life and that kind of character at all events. In comparison with busy Martha, you may think you have chosen the better part as the Marys of intellect, but after all somebody has to do the cooking even for you."

Such might well be the busy Philistine's apology for his life, and even Carlyle, who gave him a name and ridiculed him as we have seen, could still write in his praise as the typical Englishman :

" I look at that surly face of thine with a mixture of pity and laughter, yet also with wonder and veneration. Thou complainest not, my illustrious friend; and yet I believe the heart of thee is full of sorrow, of unspoken sadness, seriousness — profound melancholy (as some have said) the basis of thy being. Unconsciously, for thou speakest of nothing, this great Universe is great to thee. Not by levity of floating, but by stubborn force of swimming, shalt thou make thy way. The Fates sing of thee that thou shalt many times be thought an ass and a dull ox, and shalt with god-like indifference believe it. My

[1] *Wealth and Life*, by J. A. Hobson, p. 62 (1929).

friend — and it is all untrue, nothing ever falser in point
of fact! Thou art of those great ones whose greatness the
small passer-by does not discern." [1]

That surly, energetic face is fast disappearing,
and I regret it perhaps even more than I regret the
disappearance of the country gentry. After all, it
belonged to a human being, and now it is succeeded
by a Joint-Stock Company, between which and the
working people no personal relation can exist. I do
not deny that, separately, the directors of a Joint-
Stock Company may have souls. God made them,
let them pass for men. But as a Board there is no
saving them, and though they certainly have bodies,
they are not to be kicked. I suppose it was the successful directors who became the best profiteers during the war and the short boom that followed the
Armistice, mainly due, I was told, to the unusual
demand for night-gowns among the harlots of South
America. To judge from appearances the directors
are perfectly fitted to carry on the traditions of Victorian vulgarity, and to prove yet again that no
camel will ever get through a needle's eye. But other
people have grown as rich as the profiteers simply
by speculation and shuffling money about, and for
them there can be as little hope of crawling through
the gate of heaven, since they have done nothing at
all for their money, and their adventures in finance
have not produced one yard more cotton or one
lump more coal.

[1] *Past and Present:* "The English," p. 58 (1843).

Profiteers and speculators we still have with us, and as I walk about London and other cities I marvel at the number of inhabitants who must possess an income so far beyond the dreams of my avarice that the number of thousand pounds does not matter. Being merely a professional man, sprung from a professional family, I have never enjoyed the advantage of mixing much with the plutocracy; but let me take the evidence of one who belongs to Society by birth and position. After saying that in these days Society is mainly conditioned by finance, Lord Gorell continues:

> "Practically anyone with money can get into Society, and we have to-day far more of a plutocracy than an aristocracy — and a plutocracy is the least justifiable, least profitable form of social organism that the world has ever produced.
>
> "It makes possible position without responsibility, it creates that floating, loudly self-advertised crowd who drift from the Nirvana of the Lido in the summer to the hot-house artificiality of the Riviera in the winter — with spasms of the 'season' and the 'little season' in between. In a Socialist State, such as one day will assuredly be, such a top to our social structure will be impossible. There will be no room in that for the wasps of humanity, those who consume and do not help to create." [1]

I have quoted one who has enjoyed every opportunity of knowing Society as it is, and owing to this dominance of a wealthy Upper Middle Class it is evident that Society stands in a very distressing and

[1] Lord Gorell in the *Evening Standard*, October 11, 1928.

unenviable case. Ought we to include these wasps of
humanity in any class of English people at all? Or
must we only pray for the time when, as Lord Gorell
says, there will be no room for them? Let us leave
it at that, as the lawyers say; leave their gluttonous
kind to stew in the juice they have gathered from
others.

Again, as I wander about the wealthy streets of
London and the nearer suburbs, such as Chelsea,
Bayswater, Bloomsbury, and Hampstead, I notice
the vast number of lofty and monotonous houses,
built from sixty years to a century ago to receive
rich people with big families, but now divided and
converted into " maisonnettes " or flats. The change
is partly due to shortage of housing everywhere, and
partly to the demands of professional men and
women who will pay any rent for the advantage of
living near their work in central London. But what
has become of those progenitors who required six
or eight stories of large rooms to live in, to entertain
their guests in, and to shelter their families and
servants — those houses that promised such a stock
of descendants, *spes tanta nepotum,* as Virgil said
of Priam's palace in Troy? [1]

Even before the war a slow decline was befalling
those hopeful fathers of families, and the new houses
constructed in Chelsea, for instance, though far
more beautiful and convenient, were smaller, and
were frequently subdivided. The average of children

[1] *Æneid* II, 503.

was evidently being reduced from eight or ten to
three or four. Indeed a family of four was already
regarded as a little uncontrolled. The war hastened
the decline. Thousands of promising and well-to-do
sons were then prematurely killed. The National
Debt was multiplied by ten; our annual expenditure by nearly five. Taxation on "unearned incomes" (that is to say on savings of one kind or
another) was settled at about one-fifth, to say nothing of super-tax and death-duties. The real value of
every pound declined as prices rose. Owing to the
vast and increasing number of the unemployed,
rates increased almost in the same ratio as taxes,
and those who had lived on fixed incomes or on
dividends from investments found themselves reduced from luxury to little more than comfort, or
even to the perplexities of poverty. They submitted
rather than face the violent uprising of hungry
mobs, which might have been the alternative. But
as a class they have been driven to practise celibacy,
or, by one means or another, to reduce the number
in each family to one or two, or very seldom three.
This diminution applies to the professional and intellectual classes especially, but it is seen among the
Upper Middle, who once formed the vital vertebræ
in the "Backbone of the Country," and now appear
to be dying out, so that we must look elsewhere for
support to England's erect position.

II. THE LOWER MIDDLE

"What God hath cleansed, that call not thou common."
Acts x, 15.

If the Upper Middle Class, with its insensitive
vulgarity, mental limits, and ostentatious display,
has been the ready mark for satire, the Lower
Middle is regarded by its superiors with dislike and
contempt or indifference. In the smaller towns, it
suffers under the paralysing tyranny of the wealthier
or better educated classes above it, who dictate a
social code of iron commandments. This banker's
clerk may be nodded to, that may not; this shop
may be dealt with, that may not; this family goes
to the church, that goes to the chapel, and you may
draw the social conclusion. In many cases, as of
shopkeepers and petty officials, for instance, the
very existence of a family may depend upon the
smile of the recognized leaders in the small town's
society, and the broad road of hypocrisy must almost necessarily be trodden. It is fair to say that the
tyranny of Upper Class seclusiveness is exercised
with equal rigour upon any member of its own class
who strays beyond the hurdles of the acknowledged
fold. But the educated rebel, wrapping himself in
his own iniquity, can afford to disregard or defy the
chilly salutations or silent neglect of the inner circle.
The shopkeeper or petty official cannot afford such
a pleasure, for on that circle's favour he lives. The
charm, the gossip, and the absurdity of refined and

seclusive life in the small country town have been
described with lasting humour by Mrs. Gaskell in
Cranford.

In the great cities, such as London, Birmingham,
Manchester, and Liverpool, the Lower Middle
Classes are released from the petty tyranny of their
superiors, because they are unknown, and the contempt or indifference with which they are regarded
falls upon the mass and not upon the man. This
isolation in oblivion is an incalculable advantage
to the personal freedom of each, for he escapes the
harassing inspection and interference of the gentry.
But in the suburbs, where he usually dwells, he is
likely to lose all sense of community and combina-
tion. For it is the pride of suburban people to keep
themselves to themselves, and the Englishman's
home becomes his prison cell for solitary confine-
ment. As likely as not, he does not even know the
names of his neighbours on both sides of his little
house in the "ignobly decent" street, as George
Gissing called it. Row upon row of those ignobly decent streets extend in parallel lines that will never
meet, nor, apparently, ever end, around all our great
cities; as Ilford, Leytonstone, Southgate, Holloway,
Brixton, Clapham, Balham, Peckham, and New
Cross extend round London.

Arrogant claimants to culture have lately attached a sinister meaning to the word "suburban,"
which I find difficult to analyse. It is not solely a
question of place, for it seems to be possible not to

live in a suburb and yet to be suburban, just as a
barbaric Tartar would remain barbaric even in
Bloomsbury. The contemptuous word "suburban"
appears originally to imply a simple, ignorant, and
unaffected disposition, untainted by social para-
doxes or sexual disquisitions. It is a mind occupied
with its own little affairs, its little house, its little
family, its little garden, its little excursions into the
country; and perhaps its little chapel. But "suburban" has been acquiring a further, esoteric meaning; for I have heard an eminent leader of culture
apply it to a well-known traveller whose mind has
never been occupied with any of those objects, and
the shade of contempt implied is too evanescent to
be grasped.

But to return from the vagaries of cloistered culture to the proper meaning of words, it is clear that
the suburban Lower Middle Class must include the
multitude of clerks, Civil Servants of the lower
grades, elementary school-teachers, shopkeepers,
trade-union officials, and the rest who are sometimes described as "the black-coated proletariat."
They are the people who have nothing to live upon
except their weekly or monthly pay, but whose work
is not manual. Among them we must now include
the recently raised army of girl secretaries and typ-
ists, whom the momentary beautiful and democratic fashion in dress makes hardly distinguishable
in appearance from classes above them in income
and social position (spring, 1930).

This class may properly be called suburban, for it inhabits those rows of little houses in monotonous streets described as "ignobly decent." As I said, the higher classes are accustomed to regard them with indifference or contempt, but it would be harsh to call the people as ignoble as their streets. Their seclusiveness makes them hard to know, but those whom I have personally known were often pathetically anxious to "cultivate their minds," to acquire knowledge outside their daily work, to hear news of foreign lands, and to travel in organized parties even as far as France or Belgium. Within the limits of their incomes, they struggle as far as they can along the high road of culture, and it is to this suburban class, more even than to the inhabitants of small towns and open country, that the gramophone, the wireless, and the cinema have brought the highest pleasure and interest in mental life. To use the appalling English phrase (child of darkness out of monotony), these inventions have assisted the suburban people in "killing time," and have even diffused a certain cultivation. But the limits of weekly or monthly income are tight, and the position always hazardous. For if the income-earner is discharged "owing to reduction of staff" (commonest and cruellest excuse), or if he falls sick or dies, what is to become of that admirably decent household in the ignobly decent street?

"He that is down needs fear no fall," sang the shepherd boy in the *Pilgrim's Progress*. But the

Lower Middle Class is not down, and it perpetually fears a fall. Having reached a certain standard of respectability and comfort, it is naturally afraid of tumbling down into a level less respectable, less comfortable. It values the separate little house, the separate little garden fenced off by iron railings, the front door opening, not into the living-room as in a workingman's cottage, but into a passage with a hat-rack and umbrella-stand, the parlour with the evergreen plant in the window and books arranged in invariable order upon the round table, the family photos in plush frames on the mantelpiece, the chairs protected by antimacassars, the back room for meals (almost to be called a dining-room), the kitchen with its gas-stove, the electric lights (so saving in wifely labour), the two bedrooms upstairs, the cleanly water-closet, and perhaps a bathroom too. No wonder this class fears a change more than anything in the world. No wonder the women, to whom a home means so much, are especially fearful of a fall.

In canvassing the suburban streets at election time, I have found that almost without exception the inhabitants vote Conservative. The very word " Conservative " seems to assure stability, and it is always a safe thing to follow the way that the Upper Classes vote, for certainly the Upper Classes, as revealed in the cinemas and picture papers, could not possibly desire a change, since they have reached an Earthly Paradise already. But among the suburban

people there is always danger, always fear. Wages
may rise, but they never rise in proportion to prices.
Direct taxation hardly touches them, but the tobacco tax and the entertainment taxes are sharply
felt. Rates are always going up, and in a year or
two that will mean a rise in rent, though rent is already a horror to think of. And then there are the
children. They may not come as quickly as they
used to, but still they come. The clothes of the eldest
can be made up for his successors, but then the
eldest must have something new. So the family must
cling to what it has, for who knows what a year
may bring forth? And there are those terrible
Socialists at the gate, always threatening to reduce
respectable people to the level of dock-labourers
and dustmen! In the Conservatives lies the only
hope.

The employment of the men and women in this
class is almost invariably sedentary, and in health
and mind the class suffers from sitting down. Dys-
pepsia results from inactivity, and the girls seldom
eat enough. But the English love of bodily action
still asserts itself. Sunday walking-clubs are large,
especially in the northern cities where hills and
moorlands stand close. Cyclist parties ran out in
every direction till motors threatened to exterminate the cycle, as in America. Even in London I
have trained a pack of human hounds that met at
Aldgate Pump, drew Mile End Waste, ran through
Cambridge Heath Road, and killed in Victoria

Park. In the City at night one may meet half a dozen youths lightly clad and padding quietly along, without any obvious object but padding quietly along. Any cricket or football pitch, from a street with a lamp-post (for the working class) up to real grass near the country (for the suburbans) is eagerly occupied. A Cadet Corps that some of us founded in 1886 has always been full, though now the Government threatens its existence (March 1930). Then there are the Boy Scouts, the Church Lads Brigade, and the Folk Dancers, all chiefly drawn from this suburban class. But this is a subject rather belonging to the Englishman's main interest in sport, and here we need only remember the intense joy of the rare family excursions into the country or, best of all, to the seaside. In all human nature there is no joy to equal the joy of suburban children when first, leaning out of the train window, they sniff the smell of the sea, and then with spade and bucket run down over the beach to the water's edge.

But one has to be careful about detecting or extolling virtues or happiness among these people of the Middle or Lower Classes, or we shall have the wits sneering at us. One of the cleverest and most admired among them, for instance, has been telling us that " there is no reason to be particularly proud of qualities which we inherit from our animal forefathers and share with our household pets." He misses peculiarly " human virtues " among these common people.

"Spend a week in any great town, and the fact is obvious," he writes. "So complete is this lack of truly human qualities that we are reduced, if we condescend to look at reality at all, to act like Charles Dickens and congratulate the race on its merely animal virtues. The jolly, optimistic fellows who assure us that humanity is all right, because mothers love their children, poor folk pity and help one another, and soldiers die for a flag are comforting us on the grounds that we resemble the whales, the elephants, and the bees. But when we ask them to adduce evidence of human sapience, to give us a few specimens of conscious and reasonable well-doing, they rebuke us for our intellectual coldness and our general inhumanity — which means our refusal to be content with the standards of the animals." [1]

Well, the standards of animals and birds are not to be despised by any human being, however refined, but as this writer treats Dickens with the elevated scorn to which he is habitually exposed by the fastidious, let me take a contrary passage from two distinguished foreign critics of Dickens and the class which he depicted so faithfully:

"Dans une vieille société comme celle de l'Angleterre, dans une société ou, depuis des siècles, les coûtumes se sont lentement glissées de maison en maison et ont fini par saturer toute la masse d'un peuple, il y a quelque chose de merveilleusement uniforme dans les bonheurs et dans les peines, dans les croyances et dans les actions. Et, justement parce qu'elle est répétée des milliers de fois, cette uniformité devient poétique. Son rythme lui est

[1] *Those Barren Leaves: Autobiography of Francis Cheifer*, by Aldous Huxley (1925).

donné par sa monotonie, sa grandeur par son humilité.
Il est à la fois terrible et touchant de constater que les
hommes attachent tant de prix à des choses si communes.
' Dickens est le poète de ces champs de maisons en briques
jaunes que le voyageur, en entrant à Londres, aperçoit
du haut des viaducs.' Ces maisons ont elles aussi, besoin
de leur poète et elles, le meritent, puisque les vies humaines complètes peuvent être vécues la. ' En présence de
cette immense platitude des destinées humaines, Dickens
épreuve le sentiment qui pourrait bien être, à l'avenir, le
sentiment dominant de l'humanité, une sorte d'heureuse
liberté dans la petitesse, un respect aux yeux ouverts, une
religion sans mots.' " [1]

Besides Dickens, H. G. Wells (as in *Kipps*), and
Arnold Bennett (as in all his tales of the Five
Towns) have faithfully depicted this class in the
weakness of its fluid sentimentality and the strength
of its regular persistence. What it lacks is opportunity for adventure, and man's natural longing for
adventure drove thousands in this class to volunteer
for the Great War, if only to escape from the invariable routine. Some military critics supposed that
in war they would at the best behave like infuriated
sheep, but they appeared to fight with a solemn seriousness beyond the ordinary English type of soldier.
It may be that among this class we should now look
for the " Backbone of the Country " or the " Bul-
wark of the Constitution," and they would fight
with their backs to their front-doors against revolu-

[1] *Études Anglaises; Dickens*, par André Maurois, p. 164 (1927). His
quotations are from George Santayana.

tionary violence. But if one must criticize people so worthy of respect, perhaps one might think them a little wanting in that sense of easy-going humour which characterizes the class above them and the class below. In that half-serious irony which is so peculiarly English and pervades almost the whole of our Upper Classes and our Working Class, they are strangely deficient. They take life too solemnly for fun, and words too literally for the ironic sense. In these respects they seem to have acquired something of the Scotsman quality, though without his religion or his thrift. So that if an ironic person ventures to live among them or to address them at a public meeting, they stare at him suspiciously, as bullocks stare at a dog which has intruded into their field.

CHAPTER VII

THE COUNTRY WORKER

"Two men I honour, and no third. First, the toil-worn
Craftsman that with earth-made Implement laboriously
conquers the Earth, and makes her man's. Venerable to
me is the hard Hand; crooked, coarse; wherein notwith-
standing lies a cunning virtue, indefeasibly royal, as of
the Sceptre of this Planet. Venerable, too, is the rugged
face, all weather-tanned, besoiled, with its rude intelligence; for it is the face of a Man living manlike."

Carlyle, *Sartor Resartus*. Chap. IV, *Helotage*.

THE VAST majority of the English people are
manual workers of one kind or another. That
must be so in all countries, for it is the manual workers who produce all the necessaries of life — food,
clothing, and shelter — and without manual work
the whole human race would rapidly perish of hunger, cold, heat, or wet. Perhaps the eccentric enthusiasts are right who imagine that in a society nearest
perfection all grown-up people would share in the
manual work whether it were agriculture, cattle-
breeding, manufacture, baking, poultering, or
butchery. Such active and sociable occupations
would, at all events, save many among our Upper
Middle Classes from the melancholy of professional

reading and writing, isolation, or flat idleness; and William James's idea of an industrial conscription for youths of what has hitherto been called "the military age" ought to find many supporters among the elderly, who regret their lack of such experience in youth. In fact, the Upper Classes and even the landed Aristocracy do already exert themselves to supply their deficiency in active manual labour by fancy-gardening, needle-work, mountain-climbing (as a substitute for mining), fishing, shooting birds, and killing the larger animals.

But all these healthy distractions from excessive thought and meditation are followed for pleasure, and only by amateurs. Such might be the more strenuous pastimes in the visionary world fondly extolled by fastidious reformers — a world entirely populated by cultured gentility. During the most refined period of the eighteenth century, indeed, all these distractions, except mountain-climbing, were freely practised with good success as counteracting intellectual proclivities, while at the same time the people who fed, clothed, and housed those elegant practitioners were hardly perceived as existing.

Or they were fantastically imagined as beings of idyllic charm — rural swains and classic nymphs, denizens of the woods and groves, tender shepherd-esses and piping youths. No poet, and no painter but Morland, dared to hint the existence of so much as a pig among them. We laugh at the pretty falsity which transplanted Theocritus to our dark and muddy shires, but the ideas of our pretty week-end cottagers are equally false, and their ignorance as blank. We all know the joy of escaping into the country from the streets. We feel like that Arch-Serpent entering Paradise:

> "As one who long in populous city pent,
>   Where houses thick and sewers annoy the air,
>   Forth issuing on a summer's morn to breathe
>   Among the pleasant villages and farms
>   Adjoined, from each thing met conceives delight;
>   The smell of grain or tedded grass, or kine,
>   Or dairy, each rural sight, each rural sound."

And then perchance a fair virgin with nymph-like step may pass, and in her look sum all delight.[1]

Those exquisite lines breathe the very ecstasy of the week-end cottage. What joy it is to wake in the morning and hear again the quiet country sounds of birds and cattle, to smell the country, and to look out upon the woods and varied fields! Nearly all the recent writers upon our country life love to dwell upon such refreshing sights and sounds and smells, praising the beauty of the English countryside, for which no praise can be too high, and peopling it, in their pleasant imaginings, with peasants and labourers drawn from their memories of Thomas Hardy's humorous and outspoken people. In rapturous tones they advocate the return to nature, and nothing could be more alluring than the pleasures they depict, and the human beings whom their own

[1] *Paradise Lost*, IX, 445 ff.

charming minds suppose to inhabit the scene. They are in some measure actually inspired with Hardy's own artistic sense; for his first wife once said to me, rather impatiently, "Thomas always imagines every maid we get to be a Tess!"

If only it were all true, and the life of the country workers were touched with the week-end radiance! The country worker is hard to know, for, living on the edge of disaster, he is full of fear and suspicion. But those who have knowledge of him give us an account of his life far from radiant.[1] Ever since his utter neglect in the eighteenth century and the hideous cruelty of his suppression in the second and third decades of the nineteenth, the country worker's life has been overwhelmed by fear or paralysed by apathy.

The story of the atrocious suppression or extermination of the English village labourers by the landowners, working with the savage instruments of transportation and gallows, has at last been told, and I need add only a few sentences from the *Conclusion* of that tragedy:

"For one person who knows anything about so immense an event as the disappearance of the old English

[1] See the chapter, "The Countryside," in the thoughtful though depressing book *The Condition of England*, by the late C. F. G. Masterman (1911), who quotes from C. L. Marson's *The Commonwealth, The Ruin of Rural England* (Essex), by an unnamed author, *Where Men Decay*, by D. C. Pedder, and *England a Nation*, by R. C. K. Ensor. I would add the great series of descriptions of Lincolnshire life by the late Bernard Gilbert from *Old England* (1921) onward; some of the late Edward Thomas's books, though mainly idyllic, *The Bettesworth Book*, on a Surrey Labourer, and *England's Green and Pleasant Land*, Anonymous (1926).

village society, there are a hundred who know everything about the fashionable scenes of high politics and high play, that formed the exciting world of the upper classes. The silence that shrouds these village revolutions was not quite unbroken, but the cry that disturbed it is like a noise that breaks for a moment on the night and then dies away, only serving to make the stillness deeper and more solemn." [1]

It would be interesting to attempt to balance the iniquity of the spoliation in the sixteenth century, which created most of the great landowners, with the iniquity of the early nineteenth, which extended their lands, and laid the labourers more completely under their control. Between them the two periods brought the English country people as near mental and bodily ruin as was possible without absolute extinction. And yet these English men and women were people of extraordinary aptitudes. According to Dr. Jessop, the scholar and antiquarian of Norfolk, there is evidence that the fabric of our churches and the decoration of their interiors, the wood carving on the screens, the frescoes on the walls, the engraving of the monumental brasses, the gorgeous vestments and banners were the work of village artists. [2] And in reading Dr. Jessop's account one can almost believe that William Morris was justified in his eulogy of the guilds and cheaping-steads in years before the big landowners came to grab the villagers

[1] *The Village Labourer; 1760–1832*, by J. L. Hammond and Barbara Hammond, p. 307 (1920 Edition).

[2] *Before the Great Pillage*, by Dr. Jessop; see also his *Clouds over Arcady*, dealing with the labourers and farmers of Norfolk.

together with the lands. At all events we know for certain that it was among the unknown generations of Englishmen and Englishwomen in the country that our folk-songs and folk-dances arose, uncounted, beautiful, and spontaneous as the buttercups and daisies of their fields.

Before the second death, only a century ago, Goldsmith had lamented the deserted village; Gray had discerned the mute inglorious Milton and the village Hampden who withstood the little tyrant of his fields; Wordsworth had revealed the pathos of the country worker's life; Byron had written *The Age of Bronze,* with its terrific refrain of " Rent, rent, rent!" And during the execution Crabbe and Cobbett were speaking with the power of inner knowledge. Yet these were but the disturbing cries that broke for a moment on the night, and then died away. The transportations and hangings continued, and it was they which left their permanent mark upon the mind and temper of the countryside.

There is a district I know fairly well, just beyond the reach of the week-end cottagers from London, and indeed, it is not pretty-pretty enough for them; for it is not Surrey. The high upland, flat, unpicturesque, and usually cold, is of rather heavy clay upon chalk, but it will grow wheat, oats, roots, and ordinary garden vegetables. The land is owned by three or four old families, all but one poor, and one bankrupt. One of the owners tries to farm the land with the help of a bailiff. But most of the land is let

out by the acre to farmers in the ordinary way at
fixed or variable rents. One farmer is doing well,
chiefly because he is good at his job. The others not
so well, and one who tries to do all the labour himself, with the help of a small family, cannot make
either a decent farm or a decent living. His failure,
and the indifferent success of the others are due to
the want of labourers, or rather to the want of
money to pay the wages due.

As throughout the country, the labourers are few,
and are becoming fewer. A farmer is lucky if he can
keep three or four and pay their wages, which average thirty-one shillings a week, with rather more for
the men who look after the horses and cattle. There
is no dairy farm in the village, chiefly because the
roads are bad for conveyance to a town. Cattle,
sheep, and horses are becoming scarcer, and manure
for the fields runs short. Most of the labourers' cottages are "tied" to the landowners' estates, and
tenure is therefore insecure. Rents run from about
four-and-six to six-and-six, the amount being sometimes deducted from the weekly wage. Some of the
cottages are ancient, half-timbered, little dwellings
— what American tourists love to call "mossy bits,"
so low in doors and ceilings as to show how short
our ancestors in the country must have been. Some
landowners have recently built substantial brick
cottages that will never remind tourists of "Olde
England," but even they are too small for the large
families, and, in any case, cottages are scarce. In a

distant village the District Council, with Government subsidy, has erected a good many " desirable " cottages, which are certainly desired. But the better kind among them are rented at nine shillings to twelve-and-six, so that no labourer can afford them, and they will probably decline into homes for clerks or week-enders, while their surplus rent goes to cover the deficit on the smaller cottages rented at five or six shillings.

For the ordinary labourer the working hours are from seven to five, with a day off on Sunday and half a day on Saturday, but the cowmen and all who manage livestock, begin earlier and have no fixed time free, because livestock are unaware of the laws. Free time is often used for cultivating vegetables on the allotments, rented by so many poles at a small charge to the Parish or District Council. With an allotment and a patch of garden at his door, the labourers can do fairly well for potatoes and other vegetables, and they expend the surplus of their recent rise in wages upon having some sort of meat every day. " Always will have the very best to eat," they tell me, but they are ignorant of the best. Some of the labourers leave the farm for a brickfield, or cycle into a distant town for the better wages in the mills. There is an old saying, " The wonder is not that many go, but that any stay." And I agree that the wonder is there.

Yet nearly all tell me they would stay on the land if they could live on it. The worst-felt grievance is not so much the low wages as the shortage of cottages, which prevents marriage. In this district there are still living three labourers' family stocks who have been here for generations, and indeed have built most of the houses from one generation to another. It is thought they will never leave till the Judgment Day. Even after the war most of the men who survived returned and took up the old labouring life again. Being English in their indomitable silence and reserve, they do not speak of their pleasure in their work or of their love of the land, though I have heard one remark upon the beauty of the scene, which was not particularly beautiful to seekers after the picturesque. But though farmers and labourers seldom speak of such things, some of our recent poets have detected in them a silent feeling for nature, and a pride in their work, though both feeling and pride are very far removed from the pastoral idylls of Theocritus, Milton, or Pope.

For the farmer's pride in his work as something accomplished and tangible as contrasted with mere doctrine and words, we have the verse of Tennyson's *Northern Farmer* (*Old Style*):

"But Parson a cooms an' a goäs, an' a says it eäsy an' freeä,
  'The amoighty's a taäkin' o' you to 'issén, my friend,' says
    eä.
  I weänt saäy men be loiars, thaw summun said it in
    'aäste:
  But 'e reäds wonn sarmin a weeak, an' I'a stubb'd
    Thurnaby waäste."

And, for love of the work, and love of the English scene, remember John Masefield's lines on a farmer's or labourer's hearing of the declaration of war in "*August,* 1914":

"The harvest not yet won, the empty bin,
　The friendly horses taken from the stalls,
　The fallow on the hill not yet brought in,
　The cracks unplastered in the leaking walls.

Yet heard the news, and went discouraged home,
　And brooded by the fire with heavy mind,
　With such dumb loving of the Berkshire loam
　As breaks the dumb hearts of the English kind.

Then sadly rose and left the well-loved Downs,
　And so by ship to sea, and knew no more
　The fields of home, the byres, the market towns,
　Nor the dear outline of the English shore."

Or, again, for a farmer's love of the work and love of the land, let us take a passage from that far less-known poet, Bernard Gilbert, whose accounts of country life in modern England are written with personal knowledge. The passage is from " Old England," the first of that long series which the strange writer did not live to finish. The farmer, John Hodgson, first clears off the ignorant land-owner with a touch of a countryman's irony, and describes his labourers as they deserved:

"The secret of good management, perhaps,
　Lays all in knowing how to treat your chaps,

Most of them's mortal bad, a few is good,
And all of them has heads like lumps of wood.

　·　　·　　·　　·　　·　　·

When you know how to manage men
You're fit for farming in the Fen."

The word Fen calls up a vision of the land he
farms:

"The land! I love it! As I lay in bed
I can see each foot of it in my head;
I know where every sheep and bullock lays,
And watches them in fancy where they graze;
I know what water stands in every dyke,
Blindfold I'd take you anywhere you like;
Nowt lives nor moves but what I know about it,
What's done is by my leave, nowt's done without it;
I send the horse to plough, the man to hoe;
Nothing can grow
But I've the sowing and the tending of it:
It's my farm, isn't it?
A-course it be,
I reckon as it fair belongs to me.
I love to watch the ploughing up for wheat,
The furrows running regular, fit to eat,
All brown and mellow, straight as any arrow,
It stirs you to the middle of your marrow;
The crows behind the plough, all hungry, hopping,
The horses keeping step and never stopping,
The steam uprising from their backs to meet
Tom Burrow's frosty breath ——
It would be death
To take me from it now, I love it so;
I only ask to stop and watch things grow." [1]

[1] *Old England*, by Bernard Gilbert: "*John Hodgson*" (1921).

Perhaps that is too idyllic an example of the writer's works, for he never hesitated to tell of the hardly describable cruelty, the still less describable lasciviousness and malicious gossip of the country life. But still, there the three poets speak, and they rightly perceive the English countryman's silent love of the land and his pleasure in his work upon it. It was with real regret that, in the very district I have been describing, a countryman said to me, "The world's too quick for farming now!" And he was only a labourer, living in a tied cottage, with a host of children, the water scanty and bad, the village well befouled, scarlet fever and tuberculosis in the place, the farmer reducing his hands, and barely paying his way.

Worst of all, hanging always over the labourer's head is the fear of losing his job through offence to the squire or the farmer. I have known a labourer, a man of fifty, say he wanted to go and work on his allotment on a Saturday afternoon, but he was obliged to play with the cricket team that the squire patronized. He dared not refuse for fear of giving offence and losing his job and his cottage. I have no doubt the squire thought he was doing a kind and philanthropic thing in organizing that cricket club. He felt he was giving the villagers some of the Public School advantages which he had himself enjoyed. Similarly, when the labourers' wives at a Mothers' Meeting, arranged by the squire's wife, were called upon to contribute to the restoration of the church

in a distant village, they dared not refuse for fear
of falling into disfavour with the people up at the
House. It was a rarer case, but quite recent, when
the squire's wife complained that the boys playing
cricket on the village green did not stop their game
and touch their caps or their hair when she drove
past. But I suspect that this fear of the squire or the
farmer, above all this fear of losing the job, is
mainly a traditional fear, dating from those brutal
persecutions of the labourers about four generations
ago. A good labourer is now too scarce a living in-
strument to be cast away for a trifle.

As to the common idea that life in the country is
dull and monotonous, there is no monotony about
the farmer's or the labourer's work; for it varies
with every month, almost with every day. Compared with the mill hand's work in a factory, it is a
succession of surprises and excitements, and one
never knows what a day may bring forth. On the human side, the " pub " is still the centre of village life,
though sometimes the squire or the parson attempts
to rival its attractions with a village hall or reading
room. The " pub " is warmer and more sociable.
The conversation there is incessant, and the tone of
voice varies little throughout all the " pubs " in the
country. The subjects are limited, as the wise man
said:

> " The wisdom of the scribe cometh by opportunity of
> leisure, and he that hath little business shall become wise.
> How shall he become wise that holdeth the plough, that

glorieth in the shaft of the goad, that driveth oxen, and is occupied in their labours, and whose discourse is of the stock of bulls? He will set his heart upon turning his furrows, and his wakefulness is to give his heifers their fodder." [1]

But such a passage merely reveals ignorance or superior scorn. A conversation about bullocks is just as likely to be interesting as a conversation about books. Labourers know what they are talking of quite as well as dons or literary critics, and in their own line their education is as sound.

But the invention of the gramophone has varied the pleasures of the " pub " and the cottage by bringing the music-hall to the hearth. And now we have the wireless, miraculously conveying down to Cornwall and up to the Northumbrian moors not only the music-halls but the Beethoven symphonies and perhaps even such religious beliefs as a bishop or dean has retained. Women do not habitually relax their incessant toil with the men in the " pub," but the numerous Women's Institutes to some extent supply the want. And down the village road comes the motor 'bus, enabling the farmers, the labourers, men and women alike, to move cheaply to and fro for shopping, marketing, visiting friends, and seeing the cinemas and all the life of the nearest town at a cheap rate. Probably the motor 'bus and motors in general will check the in-and-in breeding always prevalent in remote country districts, and perhaps

[1] Ecclesiasticus, xxxviii, 24 ff. Revised Version.

the main cause of the tuberculosis which is one of the curses of village life. As I watch the motors rushing to and fro through our villages, I think that it is no longer the disappearance of the countryman that is to be feared, but the disappearance of the country.

To the intellectual advantages of the gramophone and wireless it seems we shall soon have to add the Village Colleges already started in Cambridgeshire. The cost is high — a total of £ 124,000 estimated for the ten colleges proposed in the county — and we do not yet know what they are intended to teach, or who will listen to their teaching, but the conception may signify a great change in agricultural life. Till quite lately most economists and reformers looked to small-holdings as the way of salvation for the country people. Many landowners were attacked for their narrow greed in refusing small-holdings on their land. But the advanced feeling is now against the small-holding and against small cultivation altogether. We used to be pointed to France to prove the success of peasant proprietors, but now they are held up as a warning to prove that the system implies intense overwork, avarice, and a narrow, niggardly thrift. I suppose these evils were revealed to our men during the war in France, where certainly they were obvious.

Owing to the number of casuals employed at various seasons, and to the number of small farmers and labourers who are engaged in other small occupations not on the land, it is hard to say how many people in England actually work at agriculture. The number of farmers appears to have risen since the war, probably because the rise in prices during and just after the war encouraged the landowners to sell, and tenants to buy, often to their ultimate loss. The official numbers for England and Wales together are about 250,000 farmers, 49,000 employed in gardens, etc., and about 630,000 full-time workers in agriculture and garden work. After making some allowance in the estimate of women employed, the official estimate of persons employed wholly or substantially in agriculture equals 1,100,000. But this estimate does not include 8900 woodmen, 1490 machine proprietors, and a few land agents and others. Nor does it include park or domestic gardeners. If we allow five members to a family, the total number of people depending for their living on farming (excluding the landowners) is about 6,000,000 out of a total population of 43½ millions. Let us not forget that the landowners also live in part from the land they own, and if their profits appear to be small, that is chiefly because, like the farmers, they have a peculiar habit of not reckoning profits till they have paid their living expenses and kept themselves and families.[1]

Harder to estimate than their numbers is an

[1] Figures from *Agriculture*, by H. B. Pointing and Emile Burns (National Union of Agricultural Workers, 1927).

estimate of the general character of workers on the
land. They vary from shire to shire, almost from
farm to farm. A Sussex ploughman has little in common with a Westmorland shepherd, and in the same
village you will find different kinds of nature, as in
the same street. The country-people described by
Thomas Hardy are not like the country-people
drawn by Bernard Gilbert, or the people in Richard
Jefferies. Yet all three writers knew the country-
people well, almost as though from the inside. The
tendency of refined and highly educated society is
always to idealize " the peasant," as Theocritus,
Virgil, and so many English poets and novelists
have done; and indeed it is hard to realize that
dwellers among the beauties of the country may be
no better in nature or in habits than dwellers among
the smoke and extravagance and clangour of the
town.

Let me take a passage from a sympathetic thinker
who certainly knew town and country well:

"I am indeed bound to say that despite the great differences between them and the town-workers, and the
greater general intelligence and alertness of the latter, I
admire the character of the country-folk most — their
extraordinary serenity and good humour, their tenacity,
sincerity, and real affectionateness. Even their silent ways
— though irritating at times — are a relief from the eternal gabble of the cities. Said a farmer youth to me one
day — after we had been listening for some time to the
rather cheap talk of an elderly and radical 'citizen' —
'They do talk, those towns-folk,' he said; and then after

a pause — 'them as talks so much, they must tell a lot of lies.'"

And on the next page of my friend's book, as though to confirm what I said about the secretiveness of country-people, I read:

> "The great drawback of the country-folk in England (worse here no doubt than in Ireland) is their want of initiative. Centuries of smothered life under the incubus of the Landlord and the Parson have had their inevitable effect. They never will speak their minds, or commit themselves to any action which is not entirely customary and approved by the powers that be. It may be different in other parts of the country, but here (in Derbyshire) the one answer to any question of importance (especially if put by a stranger) is, 'I don't know — I don't know.' So fearful have they been for generations lest their words should be by chance reported in ruling quarters that the habit of concealment has at last got into their blood. One sees from this how paralyzing our land system is towards all manhood and resourceful initiative in the country."[1]

Those two passages taken together give the essential character of the English country-people as nearly as two brief passages can. But whether we idealize them, or regard them with educated scorn, or simply like being among them, we cannot forget that the country-people are the truest types of our English race and from them or their immemorial ancestors we have acquired all such qualities and aptitudes as we may now possess.

And, for a final touch of English irony, let me

[1] *My Days and Dreams*, by Edward Carpenter, pp. 284, 286 (1916).

recall a verse from the old song, "Lavender's Blue," which my Somerset nursemaid used to sing to me. Ironically it describes the ideal of the farmer's life:

"Call up your men, diddle, diddle, set them to work,
   Some to the plough, diddle, diddle, some to the cart,
   Some to make hay, diddle, diddle, some to cut corn,
   Whilst you and I, diddle, diddle, keep ourselves warm."

CHAPTER VIII

THE WORKPEOPLE

"I have left till last the most important consideration — the heart to do it (i.e. to work). You may multiply the most modern of machines, you may adopt the most modern of methods, but the human element is, and will remain, the key to the situation. It is there that the economists and calculators fail. They regard men as mere machines, but it is men, not machines, who have made our Empire. Let us have a truce to party politics and political manœuvres. It is the country that matters."

Lord Chancellor Sankey's speech on the Coal Mines Bill in the House of Lords; April 29, 1930.

"The 'standard of living' in its ordinary acceptation is a distinctively material standard. It finds its justification in the truth so strongly enforced by Aristotle that we must first have a livelihood and then practise virtue."

Wealth and Life, by J. A. Hobson, p. 74 (1929).

MOST ENGLISH people get up at six or six-thirty, though large numbers still at five, and the Upper and Middle Classes not till seven-thirty, eight, or even later. Some of the working classes begin work at six, but eight is becoming more usual, breakfast being taken first. On an average all of them work for eight hours a day, not including the interval for dinner, so that if they begin work at eight, they generally knock off at five-thirty or six. These hours do not apply to the works, mills, or pits that have to be run by shifts, usually three in the twenty-four hours of day and night.

The " knocker-up " is now employed chiefly for railway workers, whose times vary. The " hooter " " buzzer," or " bull " sounds the time for beginning work. Some men carry the midday meal with them, others go home for it or get it in the works or in a neighbouring shop. Most of the cooking and baking in the North is done by the housewifes, and the quality of food is improving owing to the Co-operative stores. In a family of four thirty shillings should be spent on food, but amount yields before fixed charges or extra pleasures.

Two out of every three grown-up people you may meet in England are engaged in industry or trade, the others working at agriculture, domestic service, education, religion, the other professions, your defence, or nothing in particular. Typical English industries are textiles (cotton and wood), mining, iron, steel and tinplate, engineering and shipbuilding, cutlery, house-building, hosiery, clothing, boots-and-shoes, paper and printing, pottery, glass, wood-work, and bricks. At the present time (1930), all these industries are officially reported as slack and declining, some in extreme depression.[1] Not being an economist, I have not discovered the cause of this

[1] See *The Ministry of Labour Gazette* for March and following months, 1930.

depression, but a layman would like to have some points explained in connection with it. As a war correspondent, I was out at various fronts during the war, but whenever I was at home I noticed that the workpeople were unusually prosperous, though large numbers were fighting at the fronts or were engaged in making weapons of destruction — labours which, one supposes, come under the head of " unproductive." All were paid high wages through the large sums lent to the country by America and patriotic fellow-countrymen, who were promised a fair interest on their loans.

That seemed comprehensible, and we go on paying the interest to those trustful and patriotic creditors by enduring a heavy load of taxes. I can see some reason for the boom in our industries during the two or three years after the peace, since people all over the world wanted the materials that might have been made during the war instead of shells, barbed wire, guns, and other means of killing Germans and keeping our soldiers alive. But I should have supposed that when the deficit was filled up and the unusual wants satisfied, we might have returned to what inventive President Harding used to call " normalcy." Yet our condition suddenly fell to sub-normal, and the thermometer has not risen again. Competition of Japan and of India herself in the cotton trade with India and China, competition of France in the cloth trade, of Germany in shipbuilding and steelwork — those are comprehensible causes of decline, but I am told of a more mysterious cause behind. Economists say the root cause of our distress is over-production throughout the world. The machines are making too much clothing, too many boots, too many machines, too much flour. An instance has been given me by a serious authority upon practical economics in a great northern city:

> "Boots and shoes can be supplied by the shoe industry in unlimited quantities; cotton goods can be supplied in unlimited quantities; steel can be supplied in the same way. The use of the word unlimited is not here implied in the strictly mathematical sense, but in the sense that the quantities would be unlimited for demand among the people. If a man had the opportunity of purchasing 1000 pairs of boots per annum, as many now have, the quantity so far as his wearing capacity is concerned would be unlimited."

There are few who want a thousand pairs of boots a year, but out of ten million insured workers in England there must be a good many who want one pair a year, to say nothing of the children's boots and shoes that are always wearing out or getting too small. And yet neither the fathers, mothers, nor the children can have the boots they want, simply because there are too many boots. In the same way, a large number out of the ten million workpeople and their children want more clothes and more bread, but they cannot have either because there is too much clothing and too much flour. To the econo-

mist the problem must seem trivial, but to me it seems as mysterious as Relativity. I only know for certain that out of every ten workpeople I may meet in the north, one will be unemployed ("playing," as he would ironically say), and is fed, clothed, and housed by the unemployment benefit. This money grant, ignorantly called the " dole," is the insurance money contributed partly by the workers, partly by the employers, partly by the taxpayers; and those dignitaries who sneer at workpeople for living on it should reflect that but for the " dole " we should have been faced with violent revolution in the years since the war. The English are not revolutionary, but hunger is a persuasive agitator, especially if the hungry have been lately acclaimed as heroes.

Are we, then, enslaved to machines which *will* go on producing, like the fairy mills that made the sea salt? Can men be called slaves to masters who work too well for them and refuse to stop their service? When Byron spoke in defence of the " machine-breakers," was he right, and were they right after all? Machines have not only quadrupled the working population within the last century; they have become their masters. Not only have they created millions of men and women to be little better than living Robots, they have evolved electrified Robots constructed to carry on the labour just as well. Hard and monotonous as is the work in which no human being can take a personal interest, even that is not so terrible a curse as the blight which for the last

few years has fallen upon over a million of our
workpeople — the blight of having no work to do.
That is the greatest disaster that can befall any human creature, though our wealthy classes do not always realize it in their own case. To seek in vain for
work while uncertain of the next meal for oneself
and family is an anguish unsurpassed, and to say
that many English workpeople prefer to sit idle and
live on the " dole " is a libel upon our countrymen,
no matter how high in political or ecclesiastical authority the libeller may stand.

Close upon ninety years ago, a man of penetrating insight realized what unemployment meant. The
exact figures for the " paupers " in Great Britain on
Lady-day, 1842, were 1,429,989, not much less than
the present average of our unemployed.

"Of these successful skilful workers," Carlyle wrote,
"some two millions, it is now counted, sit in Work-
houses, Poor-law Prisons; or have 'out-door-relief' flung
over the wall to them — the workhouse Bastille being
filled to bursting, and the strong Poor-Law broken
asunder by a stronger. They sit there these many months
now; their hope of deliverance as yet small. In work-
houses, pleasantly so-named, because work cannot be
done in them. Twelve-hundred-thousand in England
alone; their cunning right hand lamed, lying idle in their
sorrowful bosom; their hopes, outlooks, share of this
fair world, shut-in by narrow walls. They sit there, pent
up, as in a horrid kind of enchantment; glad to be imprisoned and enchanted, that they may not perish starved.
. . . Passing by the workhouse of St. Ives in Huntingdon-
shire, on a bright day last autumn, I saw sitting on wooden

benches, in front of their Bastille and within their ring-wall and its railings, some half hundred or more of these men. Tall robust figures, young mostly or of middle age; of honest countenance, many of them thoughtful, and even intelligent-looking men. They sat there near by one another; but in a kind of torpor, especially in a silence, which was very striking. In silence; for, alas, what word was to be said? . . . In the eyes and brows of these men hung the gloomiest expression, not of anger, but of grief and shame and manifold inarticulate distress and weariness; they returned my glance with a glance that seemed to say, 'Do not look at us. We sit enchanted here, we know not why. The Sun shines and the Earth calls; and by the governing Powers and Impotences of this England, we are forbidden to obey. It is impossible they tell us!'"[1]

Or take a few sentences from one who was writing close up to our present time. He speaks of work as "The Blessing of Adam," and continues:

"So powerful is this innate craving for labour that it may take all the massed resources of a great public school and of a famous and ancient university to make a boy believe that real work is a thing to flee from, like want or disease, and that doing it and 'having a good time' are states naturally and immutably opposed to one another. . . . At every congress of organized workmen there seems to run through almost every speech an implication that bodily work is nothing but an evil only to be borne for the sake of the pay that it brings, and that the few poor devils who do no work but try to while away their shabby days with expensive attempts at self-amusement have got hold of an undue share of happiness, to the

[1] *Past and Present*, Book I, Chapter 1.

exclusion of everybody who is busy. Is it possible that none of the speakers has ever known the kind of pervasive benediction that seems to descend on body and mind after the first hour or two of a day's digging, house-decorating, or reaping?

"Childish as it is to think of going back, on any large scale, to archaic handwork and petty production of all sorts, still the sentimentalists of hand-spinning, hand-weaving, and hand-sewing have got hold of one truth — that there is more joy in a person who has slowly and clumsily made a whole piece of cloth single-handed than in ten persons who have made a thousand pieces of cloth between them in the same time, by the aid of several cunning machines which they only half understand.

"The caravan has to go on; to loiter at any distance behind is to court extinction sooner than it need come. Machinery and mass-production are our fate, and if they have taken the natural delightfulness of work out of a great deal of it, that was when the real Fall came and not when Jehovah told Adam that there was a great deal of perspiration before him." [1]

Certainly it is childish to think of going back, and William Morris's mediæval ideal of craft-guilds, cheaping-steads, or an idyllic life beside the upper Thames, as described in *News from Nowhere*, is no more to be realized now than a mediæval miracle. Machinery is the worker's fate, and machinery has taken the joy out of work, because it has taken the personality, which is art. Under the dominance of machinery, impersonal monotony cannot be avoided, and the factory hands have to put up with

[1] *A Writer's Notes on his Trade*, by C. E. Montague, p. 209 ff. (written *c.* 1927, published 1930 after his death).

it just for the sake of living. I should like to agree with C. E. Montague in everything, but I can hardly imagine that the condition of those few poor devils who do no work but try to while away their shabby days with expensive attempts at self-amusement is more unhappy than that of the workers in a modern textile factory, engaged year after year in the monotonous labour of managing the same little process on the same machine, and only too glad if that unvarying labour does not abruptly cease.

"Too unhappy did they but know their unhappiness," I think to myself as I watch the boys and girls, the men and women involved for life in the buzz and clatter of machines creating Lancashire cotton or Yorkshire wool. This seems to me a natural reflection, and lest dull critics should call it sentimental, I can, unfortunately, support it by official documents, from which sentiment is officially excluded. A document upon "The Effects of Monotony in Work" contains the following conclusions:

"The experience of boredom is fairly prevalent among operatives employed on repetitive processes of the type considered in this report.

"Boredom causes a reduced rate of working which is particularly noticeable about the middle of the spell. This decrease usually lasts from one to two hours. . . . It is followed by a steadier and improved rate of working as the end of the spell is approached.

"The amount of boredom experienced bears some relation to the degree of mechanization of the task. It is less liable to occur when (a) the work is entirely automatic.

In such cases thought can be detached from work and directed to more interesting subjects, or utilized in conversation with other workers. If, however, the mind is not distracted in this manner, boredom can be very intense; (*b*) when attention is entirely concentrated on the task. In such cases unexpected and varied situations frequently arise and the operative has no time to dwell on unpleasant features associated with the conditions of work. It is most marked in semi-automatic processes which require enough attention to prevent mind-wandering but not enough for the complete absorption of mental activity.

"The experience of boredom is largely dependent upon individual characteristics and tendencies. In particular workers of superior intelligence seem to be bored by repetitive work. The more intelligent operatives are, however, usually above the average in productive efficiency, while the less intelligent workers tend to be below the average in this respect. Individual differences in ability to mechanize a task, and consequently in ability to detach themselves from work, are also very marked. Temperamental tendencies are important determinants of boredom, and need special investigation.

"The amount of boredom bears some relation to the conditions of work. It is less liable to arise when (*a*) the form of activity is changed at suitable times within the spell of work, (*b*) when the operatives are paid according to output produced instead of time worked, (*c*) when the work is conceived as a series of self-contained tasks rather than as an indefinite and apparently interminable activity, (*d*) when the operatives are allowed to work in compact social groups rather than as isolated units, and (*e*) when suitable rests are introduced within the spell of work.

"Continued exposure to monotonous conditions of

work causes adaptation to such conditions, so that work which initially is tedious and unpleasant may afterwards be tolerated or even mildly enjoyed." [1]

Digging, house-decorating, or reaping may well bring that pervasive benediction of which C. E. Montague speaks, but not much benediction seems to pervade what the official report calls "repetitive processes." And yet a very high proportion of English people are engaged upon repetitive processes nearly all their lives. Workers of superior intelligence are bored by them, we are told, but if only the conditions of work become sufficiently monotonous, they may in time be tolerated or even mildly enjoyed. "Too unhappy did they but know their unhappiness," is the natural reflection of anyone whose life, owing to the luck of birth and upbringing, has been varied and easy and pleasant compared with theirs.

Foxes have holes and birds have nests, even the hermit crab protects its defenceless body by creeping into another shell. But mankind, the most defenceless of animals, has no such natural shelter. And so, by sheer inventiveness, he has slowly evolved coverts in caves and sleeping-places in forests for himself. Palaces, mansions, halls, villas, suburban streets are his best inventions for eating, sleeping, and producing children in. But most English people spend their lives in factories and in two-

[1] Report issued by the Industrial Fatigue Research Board, July 29, 1929 (Report No. 26, H. M. Stationery Office).

storied, four-roomed houses, built side by side in long rows. In many cases, perhaps in most, each house is subdivided between two or more families, and though the style of house differs a little in different districts, the houses are monotonous in each. In the East End, for instance, and in South London, where the London workers chiefly live, the houses are almost invariably of yellow brick; in the large Midland towns of red or purple brick, and in the vast congeries of towns round Manchester of red or brown brick; but a little further north of brown stone. Yellow, red, and brown are all quickly darkened by smoke, but for some reason the Midland houses, as, for instance, in Leicester, keep their colour better, perhaps because the regulations for consuming smoke or letting it fly only at certain hours are better observed. In Sheffield, on the other hand, where regulations are supposed to exist, I found the chimneys in 1929 belching thick black smoke with customary negligence.

Regulations or not, so thick a smoke hangs over the industrial north that the summer sunshine is white and the washing in Buxton is spotted, according to the wind, with the smuts from Manchester on the west or Sheffield on the east, each rather more than twenty miles away across the hills. To the artist the outlook over Halifax, St. Helens, Huddersfield, Oldham, the towns between Leeds and Sheffield, or the Black Country of South Staffordshire may be sublime in horror, just as hell may be sublime to a poet. And the outlook is easily found, for, happily for the north, and even for Staffordshire, the hills and moors are nowhere far away, and escape to them is possible, if money allows. Turning sharply left on the Rochdale road from Uppermill, for instance, a road climbs to a high point called Scouthead (perhaps from the days when Prince Charlie's romantic rabble straggled into Manchester), and thence, looking east, one sees high ridges of moorland and rock, pierced by the long valley where the pass crosses the Pennines to Huddersfield; and south-west one looks through massive smoke over the crowded chimneys and innumerable habitations of Oldham and Manchester. Similarly, from the height of Undercliffe above Bradford, one looks north-east over a bleak plateau towards Leeds and Harrogate, and north-west through the smoke of Bradford and the populated hills around the city far up Airedale to Keighley and the lonely moors where the Brontës lived.

Even one century ago the whole of the industrial north was a scene of great natural beauty, and pathetic traces of beauty may still be found, not only in the moorlands and the dales above the cities, but even in the municipal parks and gardens, frequent and large in the midst of factories and streets. Or they may be found in the old manor houses, which must have been built there in large numbers in the Jacobean time — built of grey stone in a modest and classical style, but now surrounded by mills and dingy streets. The inhabitants of those dingy streets live for a full week of five-and-a-half days on wages running up to an average, for husband and wife combined, of about 40 shillings; but in special trades the wage is higher, and a dyer, an engineer or skilled ironworker may make up to 60 or 70 shillings by himself. Rents vary too, but the average is about 10 shillings including rates. Newly built "Corporation houses" run up to as much as 15 shillings a week with rates included, and these are much sought after by the best-paid workers; also by tenants who sublet in single rooms and themselves live rent free, with a margin to spare besides. These costly homes have four rooms ("two up, two down"), and sometimes a bathroom, besides a separate water-closet. But in Leeds I was told of 72,000 back-to-back houses still let at 3 or 4 shillings for every two rooms (Sept. 1929), just like the worst type of miners' cottages in Durham.

Let us take a high average and say that a family of workers in Lancashire or Yorkshire, by combined labour, makes £5 a week in a full week of 45 hours. With steady work all the year round, the family income would then be about £250 a year, from which £25 to £30 or £40 would be deducted for rent. Then there is the insurance money against sickness and unemployment to be paid. The remainder must be divided out between food (the first necessity), clothes, firing, washing, and tram-fares. Not much is then left for drink, tobacco, the pic-

tures, and general debauchery. All such delights are further restricted by the rise in the cost of living since the beginning of the war. In the spring of 1930 it still stood at 61 per cent, and the rise in the cost of food at 50 per cent, or just half as much again. Perhaps that is the reason why a high authority upon living and its cost lately maintained that " No bachelor in London can live under £1500 a year.[1] The standards of life are perhaps different, but we see how national poverty oppresses all alike. For I myself, before the war, have contrived to live as a bachelor in London on one-fifteenth of that amount, and in the north a whole family thinks itself happy to have one-seventh.

As another evidence of the difference in standards of life, I may quote two parallel passages that appeared together in the same column on the " Home Page " of a great daily paper. The first gives an account of the workwoman's ordinary life in a Lancashire manufacturing town:

"Even though she may not do so much baking and washing as formerly, the Lancashire mother who divides herself between the weaving shed and the home still has a busy time of it. Her eight-hour day at the mill will mean starting out at 7.15 in the morning and returning home at 6. Then she must see to the arranging, the cleaning, the cooking, the nursing, perhaps even the washing. The woman whose husband is an ordinary mill-hand has no money for work to be done, and the ordinary mill-hand takes it that woman's work is woman's work.

[1] Editorial Note in the *Evening Standard*, April 9, 1930.

"While the children are young the woman must get up at six, make the breakfast, put the dinners up that are to be taken out, dress and wash the children, and then take the youngest some distance to the daily foster-mother as the last job before setting out to work. At night she must make the tea, wash in inverse ratio to her purse — which is always light or very light — cook, and between-whiles keep the house, the children, and herself clean and tidy. Ironing and darning are odd jobs. Always there is the air of trying to catch up with the work; always the incessant certainty that it is impossible."

Further down in the same column, I read advice how to make "sandwich flags":

"Little flags for sandwiches have enjoyed a long and well-deserved popularity, adding as they do to the decorative side of the table or buffet as well as warning the guests whether their favourite or most disliked mixture is inside. . . . With the revival of the cocktail parties and dances of the autumn one wonders whether the flags could not be made a little more original and amusing, and so give a certain novelty to the decorations. So olive or cress sandwiches would be given a green flag and an emerald pin, shrimp or *pâte de foie gras* would have a pink pennant and pink top, while a scarlet pin and slightly lighter label would blazon sandwiches of tomato."[1]

The official report of housing in Wigan states that "overcrowding is very prevalent, many houses being occupied by two to five families," and as instances it tells of a house with two living rooms and three sleeping rooms occupied by three families,

[1] The *Manchester Guardian*, September 19, 1928, p. 6, column 6.

consisting of five adults and ten children; a house of two living rooms and two sleeping rooms inhabited by seven adults and eleven children; a house containing two living and two sleeping rooms occupied by two families of six adults and eight children. So the dismal list goes on, and the report adds: "The major portion of infant deaths occurred in congested areas"; "Many homes are altogether unfit for confinements." And an instance is given of a woman whose baby was born (only to die) on the one bed in the one room occupied by her husband and four children. "Many other instances of impossible conditions could be quoted."[1]

When I was living among the miners around Sunderland in the middle 'nineties, their housing was even more atrocious. They lived in long and dreary streets of two-storied houses often back to back, and always sharing the pump and the outside "privvy" (falsely so called) between six or eight families. But atrocious as that was, the housing in South Staffordshire at that time was still worse, and the pervading depression of life among the "thick-coal" miners, the iron-workers, and the nailers was more profound. The conditions were not alleviated by the habit among many houses of leaning sideways or collapsing owing to the subsidence of the earth's surface as the thick-coal below was scooped out. The ordinary room in which I lived in a nailer's

[1] Annual Report (for 1928) of Dr. Henry Whitehead, Medical Officer of Health for Wigan.

house was, it is true, occupied by me alone, without other adults or children, but it had no furniture at all except a broken iron bedstead, and all washing, shaving, and other daily functions had to be done in the small yard outside, used by several neighbours in common.

Under the various Housing Acts passed since the war thousands of eligible little houses have been built all over the country in monotonous but creditable style, and the Lower Middle Classes or the " aristocrats of labour " inhabit them gladly. But owing to the expense of building and the ground-rents accruing to the landowners by the enviable process of " unearned increment," the rents of these desirable residences are beyond the means of the ordinary manual worker; and added to rent there is generally the fare to and from the scene of his work. The consequence is that in London alone, as in certain parts of Poplar, Limehouse, Notting Dale, Vauxhall, and even Westminster, one still finds families inhabiting houses condemned as " unfit for human habitation." The people go on living there either because the coverts are near their work, or because they prefer to have the rain and snow coming through the roofs to being obliged to pay rent out of their miserable earnings. In some districts, as along the canal in Limehouse, for instance, I have found the inhabitants of the worst slums strongly objecting to a clearance of " condemned " houses to make room for artisans' dwellings in flats

because the change would deprive them of their
tiny back-yards and the delight of keeping pigeons. So true is Canon Barnett's saying that we
are all governed by our tastes rather than by our
interests.

Even among the worst conditions of the North,
Midlands, or London, the miracle is that there one
may still find the cheerful irony, the kindly affection, and the general love of decency and cleanli-
ness that distinguish our heroic race even in ex-
tremes. As a writer who has known the inhabitants
of London slums very intimately has said:

> "The wonder of man in rising superior to his surround-
> ings does not entirely whitewash our disgrace in making
> them such that a really modern pig-breeder would not
> think them good enough for swine." [1]

The extension of manufacturing industries to the
south of England is likely to ruin all that is left of
our country's picturesqueness, but it gives the workers the advantage of new buildings for factories and
homes. The official report of the Chief Inspector of
Factories and Workshops tells that during the eight
years from 1920 to 1928 the number of registered
factories in the Southern Division has increased by
over 3000, and some of the new works are of great
size. [2] Between Acton and Slough, the report says,
within five years the number of factory workers has

[1] Evelyn Sharp in the *Manchester Guardian*, October 17, 1928.
[2] Annual Report (for 1928) of Sir Gerald Bellhouse, Chief Inspector of
Factories and Workshops.

increased from 60,000 to 150,000, and no one who travels along the Great Western Railway would question it. All the great manufacturing cities are similarly expanding outwards, mainly in concentric circles, and the danger is that these outer circles will again in their turn become congested, unless the schemes of "town-planning" can prevail against immediate money interests.[1] At all events, the newly constructed districts and circles have a chance of making a fresh start, as in the beautiful county of Kent, which otherwise the new coalfields will destroy, whereas in our ancient country the expense of clearance and rebuilding is an almost invincible obstacle owing to the habits of the people and the complicated interests involved. Bloomsbury, for instance, is a beautiful, interesting, and, I am told, specially intellectual district. One would regret to see it swept clean away, but it is too old for the customary decencies of modern life. Apart from beauty, interest, and intellect, the same is true of our old manufacturing cities.

Living under such conditions of housing and labour, the majority of the English people were likely to degenerate in physique, and they have degenerated. In 1925 out of every 100 men offering themselves for the Navy 90 were rejected as unfit. Out of every 100 offering themselves for the Police 95 were rejected as unfit. We must allow for the destruc-

[1] See "Outward Move from the Cities," by Vaughan Nash in the *Manchester Guardian*, September 10 and 11, 1929.

tion of nearly a million of our best men in the war, and probably in the near future we shall find that the children begotten during the war, while four or five million of the best men were away, will be below the normal standard. Some trades, too, are peculiarly unwholesome, such as file-making and glass-work. It is remarkable that the sailors of the mercantile marine and the canal bargees have a high death-rate, though so much of their life is spent in the open air. It seems that the unwholesomeness is due to the confined and poisoned air of the fo'c'sle berths and the barge cabins at night. I cannot doubt that the evil atmosphere of the workers' houses has the same effect upon the race. "What do I care for the Empire on which the sun never sets?" cried a Poplar woman to Masterman. "In our court the sun never rises." [1] And a Whitechapel boy once said to me, "What's the British Empire to me when I have to open the window before I can put my trousers on?"

Besides the want of air and sun there is the want of good food. I have travelled too much and been in too many campaigns to be particular about food. Like the young king in the ballad, I am not a fussy man. But living in the Black Country with a family in fairly regular work, I found the food always bad and sometimes almost uneatable — the stringy bread, the dubious meat, the rancid butter, the syrupy tea. That was in a fairly well-to-do family,

[1] *The Condition of England*, by C. F. G. Masterman, p. 126.

but it must be far worse when every farthing has to be watched, and children are sent out to earn their bread by waiting hour after hour in queues a hundred or two long, sometimes after walking four or five miles, in the hope of buying " stale " at threepence for two old loaves.

Having tried both, much against my will, I find that hunger and thirst are the worst of bodily sufferings, but one must also take into account the starvation of the soul. The amazing improvement in education within the last sixty years is the finest advance the country has made. But still the children of the workers leave school just at the time when the best education of the Upper Classes is beginning. As an expression of what this may mean to a boy whose parents cannot afford the better education, I will quote only a passage written by Dickens in a letter published by his son after the writer's death :

> "No words can express the secret agony of my soul as I felt my early hopes of growing to be a learned and distinguished man crushed in my breast. The deep remembrance of the misery it was to my young heart to believe that, day by day, what I had learnt and thought and delighted in, and raised my fancy and my emulation up by, was passing away from me, never to be brought back any more, cannot be written."

A man of inborn and persistent genius may overcome such misery, as Dickens did, and as did Alfred Williams, the " Hammerman Poet," who learnt the classics from lexicons, and transplanted them and,

later on, the Sanskrit *Panchatantra* into exquisite verse. But persistent genius is rare.[1]

The dress of workmen is still dingy and insignificant, but the dress of men in the Upper Classes is not much more beautiful, though seldom scrubby or second-hand. The dress of workwomen in the north has changed since my childhood. For then they almost invariably wore picturesque shawls over their heads instead of hats, and their skirts were long, concealing such stockings as they had. Now, by the democratic fashions of open necks, small round hats and short skirts showing stockings of something like silk, most women and girls look as if they belonged to the same class, no matter what their work or leisure. Bare-footed children used to be evidence of the north, but now they are rare, and the clothing of the children in the working families both north and south, is always a marvel when one remembers the wages and the rent. But I have known decent mothers who have come from the north to London and have collapsed into carelessness and drink owing to the dirt of London slums and the impossibility of keeping the children as decent as they themselves were.

Even in Yorkshire, the hereditary interest in horses and horse-racing is declining before the incursion of motors, and one may regret the change from living things to mechanisms, though charabancs

[1] For an account of Alfred Williams, a "half-timer" son of a village carpenter, see a letter from Mr. F. H. Morgan, K. C., to *The Times*, April 27, 1930.

and motor-buses have facilitated the enjoyment of seeing one hideous town instead of another. They have also facilitated visits to seaside resorts, such as Blackpool, Scarborough, Skegness, or Hunstanton. In some towns these holiday visits are periodical during the days or the week called the Wakes, the Feasts, or the Fêtes (pronounced Feets), which are the occasions of superb annual holidays. At Oldham, for instance, for the week of the Wakes beginning August 31, 1929, the workpeople, though work was running slack, had saved up £250,000 for transitory joy. All ceased work, except the engineers who remained to keep the machines in order, and by families all set off in long processions of charabancs to Blackpool, where the staple industry is giving pleasure. There, in voluptuous innocence, they paraded the two miles of flat promenade or the extensive piers, where energetic conductors showed what music is. They encamped upon the breadth of sand at low tide. They designed elaborate castles, far beyond their means. They paddled in the shallows, one child falling face-downwards in a puddle and being drowned unobserved in the crowd. They rode horses and donkeys. They were photographed in groups. They joined in the singing of the Salvation Army. They wallowed in the bathing pool. Inside the Amusement Park they made up on the roundabouts what they lost on the swings. They fired at bottles and moving stags. They consumed what the Americans call sea-food and everything eatable. Young men and maidens exchanged hats to establish the equality of the sexes, and all had " a regular do." But hardly anyone was drunk, for one of the few advantageous results of the war has been the decline of drunkenness throughout the country, partly owing to the national necessity of paying for the war by increased tax on drink.

Wakes and Feasts are much used as suitable opportunities for weddings, and in Leicester one used commonly to hear, " We've been married five years come next races "; that is next October. Tennis is too expensive for most workpeople, and so is golf in England. So is cricket — too expensive and too slow, except in side-streets with a lamp-post as wicket. But football is just right, whether " soccer " or " rugger," and the Final for " t'Coop " is to the North and Midlands what the Derby is to London. Youths get gymnastics in many Clubs. Boxing is still fairly general, and so is whippet-racing, and pigeon-flying for wagers. The tastes of the aristocracy are emulated by rabbit-coursing and the release of rats from cages in front of the terrier's nose. Allotments just outside the big towns, and even the tiny yards of their own houses, afford the primitive recreation of gardening to the quiet sons of earth. And (in South Staffordshire alone) I have often watched the athletic and exciting sport of leaping over chairs placed back to back in a row. The " joomper " plants his heels together, takes a heavy weight in each hand, swings the weight, makes two

little feints at jumping for impetus, and at the third
swings the weights hard, drops them and leaps over
the chairs. I have seen a man clear ten kitchen
chairs in a row.

Like football, racing, and athletics, religion helps
to vary the dullness of life with chapel-going, hymn-
singing, and Pleasant Sunday Afternoons. At times
political meetings with oratory, questions, disputa-
tions, and possible disturbances add a characteristic
zest. "Mine never took much to Gord," said a
Whitechapel woman, "he's more of a politician."
And besides, a love of primitive beauty is almost
universal among the English people. One sees it in
the overcrowded decorations of every home, even if
that is a single room. I do not mean only the family mourning cards arranged on the mantelpiece
and walls, but the glass and china ornaments, the
pictures of Biblical scenes, and perhaps a perennial
plant by the window. The workers' passion for nature is known to every woman who has walked
down a slum carrying flowers. "What is the most
thrilling sight you ever saw?" was the question to
a working-class child, and the answer came pat: "A
field of foxgloves." [1]

I have always felt that it is rather impertinent, if
not impossible, for a merely professional man like
me, whose life has been so easy and pleasant in comparison with theirs, to speak about the troubles, the
hardships, and the perpetual anxieties of working

[1] *The Child Grows up*, by Evelyn Sharp, p. 167.

people; or even about their pleasures and intervals of enjoyment. I have lived among the dockers and other workers in East London, among the North Sea fishermen, the miners in Durham, the nail-makers, iron-workers, coal-miners, and potters in North and South Staffordshire; but owing to the fortune of birth and upbringing I have never worked as one of them, and I doubt if anybody whose livelihood has not depended upon manual work has the right to discuss the working population. Still I may draw one or two personal conclusions.

To me the life of the deep-sea fisherman upon the trawlers of the Dogger Bank and other parts of the North Sea appeared cruelly hard. They suffered terribly from cold and wet. Almost daily someone on each of the four trawler fleets had a limb broken or an arm or finger crushed as the dinghies took the boxes of fish to the " cutter " for the Billingsgate market. For the boats jostled together on the cutter's lee, and the unloading was dangerous when there was a sea on. After a fairly good catch, eight hundred to a thousand boxes have to be shot on board the cutter and stowed below, while the dinghies and the cutter stagger this way and that, rising and falling, driving against one another, blown upon by a howling wind, and swept by blinding seas. If a man falls beneath the boats he cannot rise, for they cover the surface like ice.

There are three hauls for the day and night so

that the trawls are down for something over twenty
hours, while the boat moves at about two miles an
hour. But sometimes while the trawl is towing
smoothly along, the "otter-doors" stick fast in
binding mud, and something must give way. Perhaps the bollards give, or perhaps the warp itself
parts like cotton. Round flicks the steel hawser,
quick as a whip-lash, cutting a man in half, slicing
off his head, tossing his fragments far into the sea.
Sometimes when the masts are hung with ice, and
the wind is dashing the spray in sheets across the
deck — when the water on deck surges violently
from port to starboard as the vessel rolls, and the
men are gutting the fish with fingers so benumbed
that crawling back to the cabin they fall unconscious with the pain of returning blood — then perhaps a mass of dark water strikes the beam, sweeps
a man far away into the turmoil of the waves, or
shatters the little vessel herself, and with a hiss of
flooded fires, plunges her down into the silent
depths, carrying with her the engines, trawl, gear,
fish, and the souls of men.

Summer and winter the four fleets remain at sea,
each fleet counting forty to forty-five trawlers, and
every six weeks in rotation one trawler goes home to
coal. Coaling takes three days, and during those
brief days the men enjoy an interval of domestic
bliss. For the rest of the time the wives pay the rent
and look after the children, and I believe the arrangement is more satisfactory than the custom of

uninterrupted family life. I do not understand why the death-rate on trawlers and other fisher-craft, in spite of all accidents, is reported far lower than the death-rate on merchant ships, though a trawler's cabin seems to me quite as stuffy as an ordinary foc's'le. But at all events, our fishermen are as fine a set as the country can show, and one is proud to hear that Britain still controls 51 per cent of the world's fishing fleet, while even since the submarine campaign against us our steam and motor marine stands first with 20.3 million tons as against the United States with 10.6 million, and Germany with 4.2.[1]

One of the few occasions when Mr. Balfour (Lord Balfour) almost lost his temper and rose to something like national enthusiasm was at the Washington Conference in December, 1921, when the French rejected our proposal to abolish submarines:

"Owing to our seafaring and fisher population," he cried in slightly elevated tones, "we could protect ourselves from submarines far better than any other country, and would do it again if the proposed abolition be rejected. No other country in Europe has that population. No other country can provide that defence against submarines. It is not there. . . . The fate of our own country I look to with serenity in this respect. . . . That it (the rejection) will imperil our security I do not believe. I do not know whether all my friends around this table can speak with equal confidence of their position."

[1] *Lloyd's Register Book. June 1930.*

Less official, less responsible, but equally confident was the remark of a hairy old skipper on one of the trawlers running between Imbros and Anzac during the Dardanelles campaign. Recognizing me from old North Sea days, he informed me confidentially that " If that there Kayser had knowed as we'd got trawlers, he wouldn't never have declared war ! "

Life in a trawler is certainly harsh, often cruel, and never lucrative. But if the accidents of birth and education had not saved me from the compulsory choice, I hope I should have chosen that rather than life in a factory. It offers adventure, freedom from routine, and various bodily activities. The men, in consequence, are courageous, good-humoured, and simple-minded. Their child-like excitement over newspapers, especially picture-papers, proved to me the glory of journalism, and I applaud those who send packets of papers out to the trawler fleets every week through Billingsgate. Besides, the three days' visit home after six weeks' absence must be a repeated renewal of love, like a lovers' quarrel.

The number of wage-earners on the colliery books in the spring of 1930 was 958,500, but that included Wales and Scotland. For England alone the number would be about 650,000 or a little more. Their underground life is at least as hard as life on the sea in trawlers. They work in darkness visible. They breathe coal-dust and sunless air. Their clothes and

bodies are black. Their scalps and spines are scari-
fied till the skin thickens and hardens like bone.
Their thighs swell with muscle like the top joints of
a beetle's legs, and in the open air they squat on
their heels like frogs. Their houses are, I think, on
the whole the most wretched in England. Yet if I
had been given my choice, I hope I should have
chosen to be one of them rather than a mill hand.
They too, like the fishermen, have the incalculable
advantage of variety and adventure. Like our soldiers and sailors, they win the prestige of courage.
They, too, feel the peculiar affection for home and
family that always exists among men who may be
separated from them at any moment for ever, and
Bob Smillie told me that on an average three miners
are killed every day. They are a seclusive and almost hereditary caste, partly owing to their hours
of work and a certain family pride. I have found it
specially hard to know them well because their
language, whether in Durham or South Staffordshire, is difficult to understand, and their technical
phrases differ from district to district. Their seclusiveness makes them hard to deal with when terms
of compromise are proposed, and partly for that
reason there are more unemployed among them
now (1930) than in any other class. But they are
celebrated for heroic self-sacrifice at moments of
danger, and if the various kinds of manual workers
were to march through London, the miners would
receive the loudest applause next to the seamen.

The lot of the English people (that is, of the workpeople, who form the enormous majority) is not yet a happy one, if judged by the standards of the wealthy, the professional, and official classes. But their condition between 150 and 100 years ago was so much worse as to be almost incredible. During those early years of the " Industrial Revolution " much was written on the glories of machines and the wealth accumulating to make England the richest country in the world. " Nowhere," wrote Macaulay with characteristic satisfaction, " Nowhere does man exercise such dominion over matter." But now, with greater knowledge and wisdom, we read:

> "The men and women of Lancashire and Yorkshire felt of this new power that it was inhuman, that it disregarded all their instincts and sensibilities, that it brought into their lives an inexorable force, destroying and scattering their customs, their traditions, their freedom, their ties of family and home, their dignity and character as men and women. If one sentence can sum up this impression, we might say, transposing Macaulay's words, 'Nowhere does matter exercise such dominion over man.'" [1]

In that great and terrible History from which I quote, one reads of the oppressive and swindling Truck system (which, by the way, in spite of Truck Acts, I have seen worked in a grievous form in the Black Country, where the nail-makers were re-

[1] *The Town Labourer, 1760–1832; The New Civilization*, by J. H. Hammond and Barbara Hammond, p. 18 (first edition, 1917).

fused the thin iron bars needed for their work unless they bought so much bad bread or bacon from
the same shop). One reads of the prolonged persecutions of the early Trade Unions as "unlawful
combinations." One reads of the legal brutality
which sentenced children of eight or ten to be
hanged for little thefts; of the case of a woman
whose husband had been transported for felony
and who committed the same felony in the hope of
joining him in exile; but the judge thought it necessary to make an example and hanged her instead.
We read that at the beginning of last century little
boys of six or seven were employed in chains to
drag the trucks along the smallest galleries of the
coal mines. Girls and women were so employed, and
the trapping was done everywhere by children, generally from five to eight years of age:

> "A girl of eight years old described her day: 'I'm a
> trapper in the Gamber Pit. I have to trap without a light,
> and I'm scared. I go at four and sometimes half-past three
> in the morning, and come out at five and half-past. I never
> go to sleep. Sometimes I sing when I've light, but not in
> the dark: I dare not sing then.'" [1]

The abominations of the use of little boys for
sweeping chimneys are well-known — the terror
of the pitch-dark and often suffocating passages,
only to be overcome by the terror of straw fires
lighted below and pins thrust into their feet. If
the chimneys were too small the boy was called

[1] *Ibid.*, p. 173.

down, stripped, beaten, and forced up again. They were sent up naked because if their shirt was crumpled they might be stuck fast, unable to move.[1] Such cruelties are familiar, but the consolations offered to working people for the miseries of the state into which it had pleased God to call them are likely to be forgotten in days when the tenets of evangelical religion are less firmly held. Hannah and Martha More were two benevolent women, who put themselves to much discomfort in their endeavours to combat the ignorance and impiety of the miners in the Mendip Hills, and their methods reveal the attitude of the Upper Classes towards the workpeople not much more than a century ago. When, for instance, a woman had been condemned to death for attempting to begin a riot and purloining some butter from a man who offered it for sale at a price she thought unreasonable, the sisters were invited to establish a Sunday School to counteract the great wickedness of the parish. And in a few months they were able to report the gratifying result that many of the pupils " understood tolerably well the first twenty chapters of Genesis." [2]

Perhaps less comforting, but even more characteristic of the time was the charge written by Hannah More to the women of Shipham during a famine in 1801 :

"Let me remind you," she wrote, "that probably this very scarcity has been permitted by an all-wise and

[1] *Ibid.*, pp. 179, 183.   [2] *Ibid.*, p. 229.

gracious Providence to unite all ranks of people together, to show the poor how immediately they are dependent upon the rich, and to show both rich and poor that they are all dependent on Himself. It has also enabled you to see more clearly the advantages you derive from the government and constitution of this country — to observe the benefits flowing from the distinction of rank and fortune, which has enabled the high so liberally to assist the low: for I leave you to judge what would have been the state of the poor of this country in this long, distressing scarcity had it not been for your superiors. I wish you to understand also that you are not the only sufferers. You have indeed borne your share, and a very heavy one it has been in the late difficulties; but it has fallen in some degree on all ranks, nor would the gentry have been able to afford such large supplies to the distresses of the poor, had they not denied themselves, for your sakes, many indulgences to which their fortune at other times entitles them." [1]

Equally soothing to misery were the words of William Wilberforce, the philanthropist, whose main energies in life were devoted to the emancipation of the negro slaves. In one chapter of his popular book, *Practical view of the system of Christianity,* he explains at length that Christianity makes the inequalities of the social scale less galling to the lower orders; that it teaches them to be diligent, humble, patient; that it reminds them that their more lowly path has been allotted to them by the hand of God; that it is their part faithfully to discharge its duties, and contentedly to bear its

[1] *Ibid.,* p. 228.

inconveniences; that the present state of things is very short; that the objects about which worldly men conflict so eagerly are not worth the contest; that the peace of mind which Religion offers indiscriminately to all ranks, affords more true satisfaction than all the expensive pleasures which are beyond the poor man's reach; that in this view the poor have the advantage; that if their superiors enjoy more abundant comforts, they are also exposed to many temptations from which the inferior classes are happily exempted; that, having food and raiment they should be therewith content, since their situation in life, with all its evils, is better than they have deserved at the hand of God; and finally, that all human distinctions will soon be done away, and the true followers of Christ will all, as children of the same Father, be alike admitted to the possession of the same heavenly inheritance.[1]

One may hope that the appalling cruelties inflicted upon the working people, and the hideous wretchedness of their daily existence were sweetened or, at least, deadened by such holy reflections. But during the last hundred years the working people as a whole have lost such benefits, and, what is more important, there is no longer so great a need for comfortable gentlemen and ladies to pour this intolerable cant into their ears. The greatest miracle in our history is that the workers of those days retained the finest English qualities of humour and

[1] *Ibid.*, pp. 231, 232.

kindliness, and have been able to hand them on to the generations following. The second greatest miracle is that by those qualities, combined with courage, pride, and persistence, they have secured for themselves the vastly higher standard of life which they now possess. One of their living leaders, himself a textile Yorkshire workman, removed by little more than two generations from the lowest level of life under the Industrial Revolution, has told us of the past advance and the hope for the future:

" I am growing older," he writes, " and I want to see in the next twenty years as great a push forward in gentleness of life as I have seen come along in the past fifty years of my being here." [1]

NOTE: It sounds mean to criticize classes who have enjoyed no such advantages as mine. But I cannot help noticing the indifference of working people to the obligations of promise and engagement. Once when a colleague of my own class failed to keep a voluntary engagement, I wrote to him: "I hope you are dead, for nothing but death could excuse your absence." One could not write so to a working man, but I have often thought it.

[1] *About Myself*, by Ben Turner, p. 352 (1930).

CHAPTER IX

INTERESTS OF THE ENGLISH

I. Sport

> "The English take their pleasure sadly."

In THAT hackneyed quotation I think the French
word for "sadly" should rather be translated
"seriously." For apart from the universal interests
of food, drink, shelter, and sex, sport is the most
serious occupation of the English mind, and the
word " sport " (shortened form of " disport ") originally means pleasure, diversion, or fun. Owing to
our passion for sad or serious pleasures it has become such a popular word among us that we adopt
it for various unexpected uses. When a plant or
animal suddenly develops some queer and abnor-
mal form, we call it a "sport," as though it acted
for fun. When a man wears an unusual article of
dress, we say he "sports" for instance a red tie,
assuming that he does it for gaiety rather than as a
political emblem. Why in Oxford (and perhaps at
Cambridge) we talk of "sporting the oak," when we
shut the outside door to exclude interruption, I cannot say; for the action implies the opposite of
diversion.

And again, we call a man a good "sport" or simply a "sport," if he plays a game hard or takes considerable risks, and we say "That was sporting of him!" if he shows unexpected or dangerous generosity. We call a man a sportsman or sportsman-like if he carefully follows the rules of the game, though at a loss to himself. We habitually speak of athletic contests at the Public Schools or between the Universities as "The Sports," but, without profanity, we could not speak of the University Boat Race or the University Cricket Match as sport. One might as well describe each as a pastime or fun, which is absurd. Within my lifetime I have heard football called a sport, but I think horse-racing never is, though the papers which most explicitly describe the races are called *The Sportsman, Sporting Times,* and so on. It seems there are some pleasurable pursuits that are too serious for sport. But, on the other hand, no one hesitates to describe the hunting and killing of wild beasts and birds as "good sport," though it is serious for the creatures on one side of the game, and cannot be identified with diversion or fun for them.

So the limit or definition of sport is evidently hard to find, but when we say that sport is the chief interest of the English people outside their daily needs, we know what we mean. Sport is, indeed, the main bond or "bind," as architects say, in that pyramid broad-based upon the mass of the working people and tapering up to the apex of the Monarchy and

Court as described in an earlier chapter. In speaking of each class or stratum in the pyramid in turn, it has been necessary to mention their various sports, for apart from the sports we could have no idea of the character. But though the kinds of sport may differ, chiefly according to income or wages, the interest is widely diffused through all classes. Thousands who have never been in a boat crowd the river banks at the Oxford and Cambridge Boat Race, and boys whose only experience of cricket is a back street for pitch, a board for bat, a lump of wood for ball, and a lamp-post for wicket, will climb any perilous and illegal position to get a glimpse of a match at Lord's.

When my train once broke down outside a station in France, I told the passengers in several carriages that the most celebrated person in the world was travelling with us, and asked for guesses who he was. All the English replied "Carpentier," the boxer, and all were right. During the " Black Week " when a lot of us were besieged in Ladysmith and the Boers seemed triumphant everywhere, an English newspaper proclaimed on its broadsheet "Another British Defeat," meaning that an English cricket eleven had not made enough runs to beat an Australian eleven. And far more recently (August 13, 1928) the *Evening Standard* headed its one leader with the word "Revolution." Remembering the apprehensions during the "General Strike" only two years before, I hastened to discover what calamity impended, only to find that the M.C.C. had issued a circular concerning the l.b.w. (leg-before-wicket) rule in the game of cricket—a rule that had occupied the serious attention of the highest authorities for forty years, and dated from the first year of Queen Victoria's long and glorious reign.

Indeed, conspicious prowess in sport may influence our political life and social legislation. I remember that when the son of a rising Conservative Minister greatly distinguished himself in a fashionable cricket match, he was pleased at the knowledge that he had "given the governor a leg up." When the Indian Duleepsinhji made 173 runs for England in a Test Match against Australia (June, 1930), he converted more English people to extended liberties for India than the two volumes of the Simon Report. And when a decent and reputable woman applied for a public-house licence before a licensing committee, the chairman remarked, "As a rule I have been opposed to granting a licence to women, because they could not keep order in a public-house. But now that Miss Amy Johnson has flown to Australia . . . !" The licence was granted.

Similarly, if during the summer of 1926 or the few following years one had asked any large English meeting which Englishman they admired most and would most like to be, one or two might possibly, in politeness, have said the King, or the Archbishop of Canterbury, or the Prime Minister, or the Poet Laureate. But the enormous majority would have shouted "Jack Hobbs!" for he had made more runs in first-class cricket than anybody since W. G. Grace, that gigantic and genial national hero.

"W.G." was, indeed, the true type of our national hero, and remembering how in the 'seventies I used to watch him at Clifton playing for his native county, adding century to century, and now and again knocking the ball clean out of the ground into a neighbouring street, I can understand why cricket is still rightly described as our national game, for it is the most serious of them all. Its rules are the most rigid, it serves proverbially as the very standard of "good form," and on great occasions it is played amid a solemn silence unrivalled in the depths of the central sea.[1] Indeed, the cricket matches between Eton and Harrow, and Oxford and Cambridge are used by Society as milestones upon the annual course of joy, or as immovable feasts definite as Christmas for ordinary people, and as the solstice for our planet.

But in the favour of the common populace football bids fair to outdo the English national game, as being cheaper, quicker, and more exciting to watch. It requires less paraphernalia, and both sides are busily engaged during the whole time of play. Some schools retain private and peculiar rites for the

[1] As both at Shrewsbury and Oxford I always took to the water, I must leave the praise of cricket to a far more experienced hand: see the admirable volume, *Cricket*, by Neville Cardus (Longmans, English Heritage Series).

game, but in England the accepted division lies between Rugby ("Rugger") and Association ("Soccer"), and I will not bring upon myself the hostility of half the nation by commending one form rather than the other. The Dominions, such as Australia and South Africa, carry on cricket with success, but football is more international, being played not only in the United States (under peculiar rules) but in Germany and France. One broiling summer day, when the oxen could hardly breathe and women sat motionless in the shade, I heard a town-crier blow his trumpet in Carcassone, and proclaim: "This afternoon in St. Rémy's Mead, in commemoration of the Holy Pentecost, a grand match of Football Rugby — the men of Carcassone against the men of Castelnaudary — *coup d'envoi* punctually at three." What a people! And what a language! "Kick-off" transfigured into *"Coup d'Envoi!"* And perhaps I may mention without undue conceit that I was the first to introduce a real football and the "Soccer" rules into Germany, or at all events into Jena University. For when I went there, they used to kick about a leathern case stuffed with straw, and the only rule was to kick it whenever it came near enough. But now I am told that the Jena Eleven ranks high among the champion teams of their country.

I have already spoken of the intense excitement aroused throughout the country, and especially in the North, by the succession of contests for "The

Cup," when many thousands swarm to the amphi-
theatre at Wembley, and it is always hoped that the
King himself will be present as at the opening of
Parliament. Illustrated plans or "Cup Ladders"
showing the relative position of the various teams
as the weeks go by during the football season are
copiously sold, and far more betting is exercised on
the events than on cricket. I have even heard bets
laid on the probable prowess and skill of each man
in a favourite team, but the almost unbearable excitement of the game itself is the main attraction,
and the scene may reveal to the foreigner how deep
and wild is the energetic passion underlying the
reputed coldness and "phlegm" of our race.

Hockey and lacrosse are fine games too, both
growing in popularity, especially in the great girls'
schools, as being more suitable for girls than football; perhaps because a football is not easy to control with small shoes and pointed toes. Otherwise
hockey and lacrosse may be as hard games as football, and as likely to cause damage to any player,
masculine or feminine.

I can hardly mention with judicial restraint the
joys of all the English sports on the water or in
it. Sailing, rowing, skating, swimming — what can
compare with them? And, to adopt a wild phrase I
once read in a provincial paper, "Echo answers
'Nothing!'" At all events, I answer "Nothing!"
but I am prejudiced by long use, habit, and memory.
There is no such tense excitement as waiting for

the gun in a bumping race; no such joyful relief as
feeling the bow grate against the stern of the boat
in front; no such sense of mastery as when the
rudder leaps and pulls in the hand like a big fish,
while the water foams at the bow and gurgles over
the side, and the sail almost dips with the slant.
To swim far out among the supporting waves, to
skate over the clear ice upon Christ Church meadows or down to Abingdon almost without a break
except the risky jump under the Thames railway
bridge — men and women are unfortunate who have
not known what that means. To drive the round
coracle with its single paddle, or the long punt with
its single pole — the instinctive skill of it, the unconscious watchfulness, the smell of the river water
and the meadow banks — those are pleasures and
diversions delightful to the English race, and open
to many, though too few. As to the more elaborate
and expensive forms of water-sports, I suppose the
English came first in the design of sails and shapes
for racing yachts, and remain unrivalled except by
the United States. And I suppose the English were
the first to invent the outrigged boat, the sliding
seat, and the smooth, rounded, keelless bottom of
racing fours and eights. On the ice, too, they have
hitherto been distinguished by their quiet contempt
for showy tricks, and their retention of the sweeping curves on the edges, or sudden reversals from
edge to edge. The construction of ice-rinks is improving the average standard of skating in the

country, but one may hope the English manner will be upheld.

Gray, Byron, Wordsworth, and Ruskin revealed to us the glory of the mountains, and a host of good writers — Leslie Stephen, C. E. Montague, Geoffrey Young, and so many more — have revealed the joys of climbing them. What heights from Scafell to Mount Everest have we not attempted? What precipices and valleys from Wastdale to the Matterhorn and Kazbek are not scattered with our bones? Mountaineering is a sport that attracts the English nature irresistibly, and it is merely a question of income and expense whether the climber cuts his way up the Weisshorn or scrambles for a Sunday over Kinderscout or Helvellyn. Indeed, the bands of "Ramblers," young men and maidens, who, with knapsack on back and staves in hand, set out on Saturday afternoons, to wander upon moors and dales, careless where they sleep or what they eat, are following sport with English zeal just as much as the athletic parties who rise from the hut before dawn, and with guides, ropes and axes creep up the slopes of snow, clinging by fingers and toes to precipitous fronts of crag.

The gentle, noiseless "push-bike" is being rapidly driven out by rushing motors and motor-coaches, noisy and ungentle, as it has been exterminated in the United States, except for the use of a few coloured people in the Southern States. But the motor-cycle, with its " peach-perch " for the girl, takes the place of a bicycle made for two, though like Robert Bell in one of his " Afterthoughts," I often think:

> " Is life, I wonder, worth the while
> At sixty seconds to the mile? "

For quiet and comparatively motionless but skilful sports, curling and golf have invaded us from Scotland, like James I's uncouth courtiers, and golf has monopolized much of our land. But our own national sport of skittles is declining, and the ancient game of loggats is known, I believe, only in one village of Norfolk and on the Shakesperian stage.[1] European nations have borrowed our word for boxing, and have always esteemed it peculiarly characteristic of English brutality! But, none the less, a Frenchman, as mentioned above, once reached the pinnacle of fame by his skill in it, and the sport has been highly cultivated in the United States, where negroes have so greatly excelled that a white opponent has been hailed with racial anxiety as " The White Man's Hope." And racquets, tennis, fives — what splendid games! And how naturally absorbed by the English, even when they originated in foreign parts!

War was called the " sport of Kings," but I think horse-racing was called so too. At all events it is expensive, and, like a war, it occupies the mind of

---

[1] "Did these bones cost no more the breeding, but to play at loggats with them?"—*Hamlet*, Act V, Scene 1.

nearly the whole nation. Derby Day is a feast more honoured in the observance even than the Boat Race, and upon the Epsom Downs one may realize that the caricatures of Rowlandson and Cruikshank still hold good of the English people in parts. There you may behold, like returning ghosts, the exuberant men in variegated hats and expansive waistcoats, across which the gilded watch-chain is looped like an Atlantic cable. There are the large-faced women, swelling in exuberating curves above the waistband and below; the loud-voiced dealers in chance, whose right hand has not lost its cunning, nor has their left. Where do they all live except on Derby Day? Sometimes such a woman has passed me like an eclipse in Commercial Street or Gray's Inn Road. But neither the women nor the men belong to the present English people. They are ghosts clinging to the exuberant life they knew in the rollicking, spitting, swearing, drinking days of Smollett, Fielding and those who inhabited our land before the decline of Old England began, as foreigners assure me it began just a century ago. But if those foreigners want a glimpse of their "dear Old England," I still could discover it for them at Epsom.

Then there is the pleasure of chasing, hunting, stalking, shooting and alluring living beasts, birds and fishes for the diversion of killing them, and this pleasure is the most distinctively called "sport." The subjects of this sport are various, from elephants to rats, but in England the choicest are deer, foxes, grouse, pheasants, partridges, duck and a few other "game" birds. Hares and rabbits are useful for shooting or coursing, and rats are coursed for five leaps on a poor-man's ground, such as Wormwood Scrubbs. Large sums are expended upon the more select forms of this pleasure, including the payment of keepers to feed the pheasants up to killing point, and to save them and the grouse and partridges from being killed by any but their rightful owners. But so deeply planted in the English nature is the lust for causing death that men will risk imprisonment and murder rather than be deprived of its satisfaction. And so contradictory is the English nature, as we have seen, that the Lincolnshire popular song toasts with equal enthusiasm the landowner and the poacher who illegally shares the sport with him.

It is another notable contradiction that our sportsmen are not necessarily cruel people. The old chronicler relates that William the Conqueror "loved the tall deer as their father," though he laid out the New Forest for their chase and slaughter. Our sportsmen show the same puzzling trait. I have known a great sportsman who hunted stags so persistently and studied them with such affection that he grew to look like an elk. And I have known another who pursued wild sheep all over the world with a similar result. To learn the habits of beasts and birds is probably to love them. And so perhaps the poet's line is true: "Yet each man kills the things he loves."[1]

Another proof of the English "sadness" or seriousness in sport is the amount of space given to it in our most serious newspapers such as *The Times*, *The Manchester Guardian*, *The Morning Post*, and *The Observer*. Nearly every day (*The Observer* on Sundays) they give up at least two and sometimes four full pages to the record of the previous day's sports, and prognostications for the future. On those pages their circulation largely depends, as is shown by its reduction if, in a spasm of Puritanism, the proprietors omit even the betting news. And what sells an evening paper next best to an aristocratic scandal or the murder of a girl is the broadside, "All the Winners." Every working man turns first to the sporting news in his daily paper, for he has always a chance of making an honest penny to supplement his meagre wage, and betting prevails in all classes, except perhaps the upper middle. As a highly-educated friend once said to me, "To have 'something on' gives the much needed spice to one's morning paper, and makes breakfast endurable."

A similar off-chance kindled the enthusiasm of the working classes for "The Dogs" in 1928. For apart from the betting there can be no sufficient interest in watching greyhounds pursue an electric hare along a regular rail, beautiful as the movement

[1] *"The Ballad of Reading Gaol,"* by C.3.3., verse 7.

of a greyhound is. Almost any competition in any kind of sport may become a subject for betting, but in England I have not heard of such a competition as I found recorded in *The Chicago Herald and Examiner — A paper for People who Think* — of Sunday, November 24, 1929. For there we were informed that James Parks of Belle Plaine won a 100 dollar (£ 20) prize for his dog, which beat all competitors in the number of fleas discovered upon it, namely 113.

I have said enough to prove that sport is the first interest of the English people, apart from the universal necessities of life. It is the bond or "bind" between all classes, and the subject of conversation in which all can take part without distinction of rank or property. Among masters and boys at the Public Schools, among the dons and the undergraduates at the Universities, and among the highest and lowest classes of the people it forms the staple of conversation. Sport is almost the only subject, except scandal, that is not tabooed by the rich and great as "high-browed" or as "shop." Foreigners might expect intellectual subjects to be discussed by intelligent people like the English, and "shop" is sure to be of vital interest since it concerns livelihood. But among the highest and lowest, intellectual or professional conversation is regarded as "bad form"; and sport is not reckoned intellectual, being a ground on which all minds can meet in comfortable equality. And as to vital interest, during the Test Matches against the Australians in 1930, news-bills announced "Wicket. Latest" on the state of the pitch like bulletins on a King's health.

II. Politics

> "This (our liberty) is that which hath rarify'd and enlighten'd our spirits like the influence of heav'n."
>
> Milton's *Areopagitica* (1644).

Next to daily needs and sport, the most widely diffused interest among the English is probably politics. Within the last thirty years politics have become more and more closely connected with daily needs, and so it is possible that in the next few years their interest may even surpass the interest in sport. They may involve the main question of life or death for most people, and everything that a man hath, even sport, will he give for his life. The whole tendency of modern politics is towards the social problems of work and livelihood for the majority of men and women — problems that did not so greatly occupy the attention of the aristocratic and middle-class politicians who controlled our government before the beginning of this century.

One may trace the change to the stirring of social thought in the 'eighties and 'nineties, when the groups known as Socialist, Social Democratic, Fabian, and Communist-Anarchist began to be organized, and the rapid advance of the general movement within the last thirty years may be estimated by the growth of the Labour Party in the House of Commons. For at the election of 1900 the Labour Party won 2 seats, and at the election of 1929 it won 287 (including 36 for Scotland), out of the 615, though no Communist was returned. The sudden growth in the last-named election (from 151 in the election of 1924) is all the more significant because the Labour Party in England had only one daily paper, and only one official weekly, both good but both poverty-stricken; whereas all other papers, with their enormous wealth and circulations, stood opposed to them.

This remarkable result seemed to disprove the idea of some editors and newspaper proprietors that the public interest in politics was diminishing, but the idea persists. For many years past the cheapest and most popular papers have been reducing their leaders, especially their political leaders, so much in number and length that the occupation of serious leader-writer has seemed likely to go. If one turns up the files of the papers of forty or fifty years back, one sees how much longer and more serious the political leaders of that age were. Three or four of the most weighty and expensive daily papers still retain the political leader upon their opening columns, and, for Sundays, Mr. Garvin's leaders in *The Observer* do not fail in length or vehemence. But as a rule the former function of the political leader has been handed over to the other weeklies and

the monthlies. Even these are little read by ordinary
people, and, indeed, the influence of the monthlies
is fading away. The most popular papers rely for
their favour upon pictures of sporting or fashionable
events, and girls in bathing costumes. But to all
this alluring sweetness they add the necessary as-
tringent taste of social, semi-theological, or literary
discourses contributed by famous ecclesiastics or
distinguished amateurs, who serve as useful black-
legs in supplementing the journalist's slighted trade.

The mere size of a paper's circulation is likely to
reduce its political influence, since it seeks to please
the average of several hundred thousand readers.
And what seeks to please so large an average can
seldom be very definite in regard to vital subjects,
as is seen in the vast syndicates of American papers.
It was chiefly by imitating American models that
the great development of English journalism was
effected, beginning in the middle 'nineties. Enter-
prising proprietors then perceived that the day of a
" Paper written by Gentlemen for Gentlemen " was
over, and directors of companies and syndicates,
acting in the interests of their shareholders, rightly
recognized that the average slightly educated man
or woman most enjoyed brief paragraphs on
fashions, sports, bloodshed, and scandals in High
Life, upon all of which subjects " copy " was copious
and easily procured. But in spite of all these temptations to more charming and personal affairs, the
interests of the English in politics has persisted, and

it repays even the cheapest and most widely cir-
culated of morning and evening papers to allow a
headline on politics now and then to emerge.

A distinguished writer in high Society, consider-
ately pleading the cause of popular papers and the
average readers, who so unselfishly enjoy the bright
reflections of a gaiety supplied them from above,
has justly remarked:

> "A certain amount of gay irresponsibility is good and
> normal. I suppose the activities of some human butterflies
> cannot be very bitterly resented by the public at large
> (who are often, I think wrongly, depicted as grinding their
> teeth with envy) or the papers illustrating their doings
> would not circulate so widely." [1]

That is true. We have already noticed that very
little hostility is aroused in this country by the
activities of our human butterflies. In other countries it has been otherwise, as once in France and
lately in Russia. But here even the reflected and
pictured brilliance of gay irresponsibility soothes
and delights the men and women who can never
hope to share its joy. Religion has been called the
opium of the people, and the distant prospect of
Society's "doings" appears to act upon us with
similarly delicious effect. In that case, we may hope
to avoid the device used in former generations for
the maintenance of dynasties and ruling classes so
as to divert popular attention from revolutionary
passions — the device of external war. The mere

[1] Lady Margaret Sackville in *The Evening Standard*, October 18, 1928.

display of Society's "good and normal" gaiety will serve as well, and cost much less in lives and taxes.

In spite of these vicarious delights and the prominence given them in the newspapers, our interest in political life remains strong, and an eloquent politician with something definite to say will fill a public hall as surely as a human butterfly however radiant. Certainly the interest ought to have increased since the Great War that was to make the world safe for democracy. For the English is one of the few democracies that have survived it. Our form of democracy has even been widely extended by the inclusion of all grown-up women as voters (1928). Ten years earlier women had at last been admitted to a limited suffrage after a long and embittered struggle against the natural prejudice of males and the obsolete sentimentality of chivalry, so that the election of 1929 embodied democracy almost in its highest possible development. The interest in politics ought to have increased in proportion, for the root principle of democracy is Justinian's saying, repeated by our Edward I, that "what touches all must be approved by all."

The principle is impossible of literal fulfilment, especially among the English, who are by nature endowed with diversity of temperament and a spirit of contradiction. But our democracy implies a government by the majority of the House of Commons, representing the majority of the electorate, which for Great Britain, Northern Ireland and the

Universities counts as 28,502,265 voters, or for England alone about 24,000,000. It seemed natural to the sporting English mind that the mass of voters should divide themselves into two opposing parties or sides, as in a battle or at cricket and football. For many generations both Houses of Parliament were so divided, though the wealthy and landowning class always predominated in the House of Lords. But, as we have seen, during this century a third party has entered the field, and it puzzles us all to discover how to conduct a battle or a football match when three sides are engaged. Our minds, though far from logical, refuse to accept so chaotic a contest, and we must remain uncomfortable until the perplexity is unravelled.

The confusion is at present (1930) increased by the sub-division of all three parties into at least two groups apiece, so that combined attack or defence is impossible on any of the three sides. Even the "Conservatives" or "Unionists" (both of which names are now as unmeaning and should be as obsolete as "Tories"), who are by nature the most homogeneous party since they most fear change for the country or themselves, are now rent asunder by a social and financial question which we all hoped had been lying quiet in its grave these eighty years, but was only buried alive. The Liberals, whose candid friends the Radicals have departed this life, are paralysed by personal and financial disputes, and stand shivering because a third party

has meantime stolen their dress-clothes. The Labour
or Socialist party, again, is divided into three or
perhaps four groups — the main or Parliamentary
party, following the authorized lead of the present
Prime Minister (1930), a man of fine personality
and the opportunist resource needed in an ancient
and traditional country; his Left Wing, repeatedly
prodding their leader from behind in the hope that
he will follow them, like cowherds who hurry their
cattle but want to walk in front; and the supporters
of the party's man of genius, who applaud his mockery of democratic government in *The Apple Cart*,
and aim at substituting the benign despotism of
" experts " almost as wise and efficient as the drama-
tist himself.

The Communists would hardly wish to be
counted as a group in the Labour party, for they
are not democrats, but, being sick of our democracy's gradual and evolutionary methods, they
would abolish our Parliamentary forms in favour
of a close oligarchy on the Soviet model. Hitherto
they have been quietly confronted by the massive
inertia of the English nature, deeply attached to the
guidance of practical experience or tradition, and
bearing no resemblance to the theoretic and widely
discursive mind of Russians. Such is the confused
condition of English politics at the moment. It is
the testing time for the democratic or Parliamentary
form of government which the race has patiently
evolved step by step through nearly seven centuries

from the "Model Parliament" of Edward I. It is now threatened by the claims of two well-meaning tyrannies — Fascism under a Mussolini on the one hand, "advancing over the putrefying corpse of Liberty," and Soviet oligarchy under a Stalin on the other, advancing over the putrefying corpses of the upper and middle classes.

It is a well-known saying of Heine's that the Frenchman loves freedom as his mistress, the Englishman as his wedded wife, the German as his grandmother. The world has changed in the generations since Heine saw it, but the English still regard freedom as the natural, legal, and accepted condition of their daily, personal lives. Freedom is not so much their "better half" as their very self. They are unconscious of it, just as a healthy man is unconscious of all the delicate and amazing processes of sense, circulation, digestion and the rest which go to make up his health. But when disease encroaches or obstructs, then he learns what health may mean. So English freedom is hard to define, and, being so long accustomed to it, we go quietly on our way without definition. It may not be true that, like the camel in the famous failure to define, we know it when we see it, but we know it when we do not see it, and then the trouble begins.

During the Great War, under the stress of national and personal peril, the English abandoned much of the freedom they had won by centuries of conflict. To the credit of the House of Lords, it may be said that, but for the Lords, we should have abandoned more. During those terrible years traditions were obliterated and the individual sank. "Government without the consent of the governed," said Swift, "is the very definition of slavery,"[1] but during the war the great majority consented to their slavery. In the hope of preservation, we handed over our freedom to Councils of Defence, Ministers, Admirals, Generals, and innumerable officials, who were the State, "the Great Leviathan," that "Mortal God" extolled by Hobbes in his reasoned defence of despotism. But since the Great War for Liberty was won, personal liberty has vanished in many European nations, and among the English people it has declined. Persecutions and oppressions abroad which would have roused a storm of pity and indignation in this country before the war, now pass unnoticed. Freedom is hardly mentioned, and stirs no enthusiasm even among our most advanced politicians. Indeed, the Labour party seems rather more indifferent to "the rights of the subject" than the other two parties, which together would represent a majority of the English voters.

For four or five generations past we have identified our English form of democracy with freedom, and it is probable that in England Parliamentary democracy will survive. But if it escapes the fate of the other European democracies which have yielded

---

[1] "Freedom consists in a people being governed by laws made with their own consent; and slavery in the contrary." The *Drapier's Letters*, VI (1723).

to bellicose despots or dictatorial oligarchs, it will be driven somehow to solve the problem of recovering personal freedom and at the same time maintaining the State. Though the war and subsequent reactions in other countries have disparaged the ideal of freedom among us, the natural and historic bias of the English is towards personal freedom, and "Every Englishman is an Anarchist at heart." It is interference that he abhors. As an English soldier expressing the common thought said to me at one of the fronts in the war: "It isn't work we mind, or fighting we mind. What we can't abide is being badgered about." The exact word was not "badgered" but an equivalent.

"The Kingdom of God is within you." The development of each personality to the full extent of its powers and its consequent happiness (since happiness lies in the exercise of powers) — that appears to be the final object of life. It is the inner kingdom that counts. The happiness of each man and woman in the expansion and exercise of powers is the object of all our political and social striving. But, unless the individual chooses the top of a column or some cave unknown where human foot has never trod (to quote an ancient hymn), he cannot escape the State, and so inevitably many difficult questions arise. Does freedom, as some modern thinkers maintain, consist in identification with the State? Is acquiescence distinguishable from a lethargy which would make all change and progress futile? If acquiescence

in the State implies torpor, at what point is protest
or rebellion permissible? Laws are rough-and-ready
summaries of convenient habits and English people respect the laws as useful guides, finding them
as a rule administered justly and without corruption. But may not a time come to disobey laws
imposed upon the inner kingdom by outside
persons or forces? How else can the individual
remain master of himself, entrenched in that
separate region which is called the Kingdom of
God?

These obvious questions may at one time or another arise for answer in anyone's life, but are more
abstract than needed for daily solution. More immediate and imminent for the English is the political issue between "the possessing classes" and the
working classes. The social questions which under-
lay the political surface of the last two centuries
have now risen to the political top, and demand
our first attention. As is natural, the generous and
well-disposed among the possessing classes consider
that the half-educated workpeople should be guided
and controlled by men like themselves — men of
weight and influence, experts in the law, and owners
of property, having "a stake in the country." As a
rule, they can count on the support of the educated
and cultured classes, professional people, bankers,
and clergy. All agree in a natural shrinking from
association with fellow-countrymen whom they regard as ignorant, unmannerly, possibly savage, and

hard to understand in thought or even in language. It surely must be for the good of the country that such people should be governed by those who have been endowed more plenteously with knowledge and experience. It is evidently for the good of such governors, who are a superior caste, like the Brahmins of India, far removed from the "Untouchables."

On the other side, we may imagine the working people retorting: "So far we have seen the nation of which we form at least ninety per cent taking her laws, traditions, and habits from you. You have set the tone, as you say, and the whole country has done its utmost to imitate you. For giving us the advantage of your guidance and edifying example in life you have taken for yourselves all the finest pleasures, the freshest air, the best food and drink, the warmest and prettiest clothes, the largest and most comfortable houses. By these means you have made yourselves the tallest and handsomest men and women. You play the best games; you run the best horses and cars; you travel to the pleasantest places; you can if you like read the best books and look at the best pictures. Such a division of happiness seems to us unequal, and we think it can't be altogether right. We are beginning to doubt whether you ladies and gentlemen are worth preserving!"

I suppose that doubt is not often expressed, but it lies at the root of all modern political and social

speculation. Are ladies and gentlemen worth preserving? We have tried to realize how attractive
many of them are, how healthy and athletic, how
adventurous and polite, how fond of animals,
and what good shots. Some, too, are so kindly,
so sensitive, so cultured, and even artistic. They
must be worth a good deal, but their price is
high.

As I noticed in a previous chapter, our ladies and
gentlemen are not detested up to destruction point
in England as they have been elsewhere. Far from
it. Most of them are not only envied, but admired,
imitated, and in some cases respected. When we
consider the wide interest taken by the working
people in the doings and appearance of Society, not
only in the divorces, but even more in the marriages,
the parties, the Courts, the balls, the games, to all
of which Society devotes so much thought and
energy; when we further consider the massive, pas-
sive force of the Law Courts, with their reverend
judges and efficient police; the army and navy,
with their officers, usually so attractive and popular; the House of Lords, still subsisting in spite of
shocks; the land-laws and game-laws, still subsisting in spite of reason, we may realize how inevitable
is the gradualness of revolution among the English
people. We are told the object of all social and
political progress is equality, but very few among
our fellow-countrymen seem in a hurry to reach it,
and even our intelligent women remain deaf to our

keenest foreign critic's advice,[1] as noticed in the
Third Chapter.

All our political parties aim, if we may give them
credit, at building in England that celestial Jerusalem spoken of by William Blake in his too familiar
poem. And yet, after all their efforts this way and
that, another poet's comment is unhappily true.
It is called:

BLAKE: A CENTENARY NOTE

"We've petrol pumps, both red and blue;
   Electric hares and putting greens,
And charabancs for fifty-two,
   And Tubes, and cigarette machines:

We've telephones and cinemas,
   P.R., 'The Sobster's Magazine.'
And Parliament and poison-gas,
   And battle-ships, and Bethnal Green.

And yet (that's just a few of them —
   The mighty schemes we have in hand)
We have not built Jerusalem
   In England's green and pleasant land." [2]

III. RELIGION

"Oh, the Jew findeth scholars! certain slaves
   Who touched on this same isle, preached him and Christ;
And (as I gathered from a bystander)
   Their doctrine could be held by no sane man."

Robert Browning; *Cleon.*

[1] In Mr. Bernard Shaw's plea for equality in *The Intelligent Woman's Guide* (1928).

[2] *Afterthoughts*, by Robert Bell, p. 29 (1929).

Nothing is so hard as to estimate a modern Englishman's religion. It is asserted that at one period of our history people actually paraded their religion, calling themselves or their children by Scriptural names, conversing in the language of the Authorized Bible, and praying or singing psalms in the open street. I can hardly believe it. If there is one thing an Englishman will not do now, it is to show his religion in public. The Salvation Army may seem an exception, but the Salvationist is supported by the enthusiasm of a group, and his religious display is recognized as customary. In church or chapel a few Englishmen and most Englishwomen will join in community singing of familiar hymns. But there, again, the natural shyness is cloaked by numbers and use. What one would expect to see in a religious nation would be a King or a Lord Mayor or a Master of Foxhounds painted for a presentation portrait on his knees in prayerful adoration, or chanting the psalms to himself. In other nations such portraits at one time appeared the natural thing, and one of the very earliest portraits of an English King (Richard II) represents him in prayer, surrounded by a cloud of lovely blue saints and angels. No such portrait was painted of Queen Victoria or Edward VII.

Our upper classes in the eighteenth century were not particularly religious. There seemed no reason for religion among ladies and gentlemen so self-satisfied, well-dressed, elegant, and comfortable.

As we have seen, the Countess on her copious tomb-
stone at Little Stanmore is described as "religious
without enthusiasm"; for she behaved decently,
and never demeaned herself to the extravagances
of those Wesley people and the lower orders. But
on Sunday mornings, followed by a negro page
carrying a large Prayer Book bound in crimson
leather, she walked down the avenue to the church
where Handel's memory was still fresh, and sat in
the Family's Box to hear the service on Handel's
own organ, followed by a sermon from a black-
gowned divine in curly grey wig reaching over his
shoulders. She was not enthusiastic about it, but
nobility had its obligations, and it was only right
that the villagers should see a good example set by
their betters.

She lived in the period most typical of the English
Church by Law Established, founded, as one of
the critics said, upon "a Patent during pleasure of
the State." [1] The Church had survived the Puritanism which lies deep among the violent contradictions of the English nature, and could look back
with cultivated scorn upon the zealots of the spirit:

> "A sect whose chief devotion lies
>   In odd perverse antipathies;
>
>   . . . . ..
>
> That with more care keep holiday
>   The wrong, than others the right way;
> Compound for sins they are inclined to

[1] Dryden's *Hind and Panther:* I.

By damning those they have no mind to,
Still so perverse and opposite
As though they worshipped God for spite." [1]

The Established Church still retains something of that quiet and unenthusiastic tone, fastidiously scornful of ecstasy, or at least of its public exhibition. It remains "the decent Church that topp'd the neighbouring hill," and the powerful or exquisite beauty of its ancient buildings scattered far and wide through the country hardly expresses its character so nearly as the semi-classic edifices of the seventeenth or eighteenth centuries, seen to perfection in the City of London, as in St. Paul's or St. Andrew's Undershaft. As a sensitive writer has observed:

"I have my Anglican moments; and as I sat there that Sunday afternoon, in the Palladian interior of the London Church, and listened to the unexpressive voices chanting the correct service, I felt a comfortable assurance that we were in no danger of being betrayed into any unseemly manifestations of religious fervour. . . . But to pay our duty to a highly respected Anglican First Cause — undemonstrative, gentlemanly, and conscientious — whom, without loss of self-respect, we could decorously praise." [2]

The satire is natural, and the writer naturally chooses a Palladian church in the City for its exercise. But set him in one of the great cathedrals or one of the ancient village churches, and a dif-

[1] Samuel Butler's *Hudibras:* I.
[2] *Trivia*, by Logan Pearsall Smith, p. 128.

ferent kind of emotion would arise. The service is still correct and orderly, undemonstrative and conscientious, but he is now in the building that has served the souls of so many English generations, and has grown from form to form like the race itself. He is hearing the actual words adapted from the older Latin use by Cranmer or some other master of language in Shakespeare's century. Satire falls away. No matter how pompous the Dean or how unilluminated the preacher, satire falls away from one who since childhood has listened to those traditional words, and still follows the simple ritual as by instinct, standing, kneeling, and repeating the well-worn responses without effort or consideration. Around him are the tombs of Crusaders and women who passed on to him the torch of English life. Above his head droop the tattered flags of English regiments, inscribed with the names of remembered or forgotten battles. In the windows glow subdued or brilliant fragments of the glass left undestroyed by the barbaric incursions of his own race — his own equally with the priests and knights and the indistinguishable coffins under the grassy mounds outside. I do not know whether tradition alone can inspire religion, but in such a scene and among such sounds the emotion of history and life-long association may be very deep.

It is argued that the beauty of these old buildings and these old services is derived from another form of religion, differing in some important respects

from that of the Anglican Established Church. And
it might be suggested, though I have not heard it
suggested, that a proportion of our ancient cathedrals and village churches should be returned as an
act of justice long overdue to the older form which
created them. We in England are not exposed to the
absurdity of maintaining two "Protestant" cathedrals in the midst of a Roman Catholic population,
as Dublin does. But still, we have a good many
cathedrals, and if we handed back, let us say, Durham, Lincoln, and Exeter to the original possessors,
we should, it is true, have to confront the full force
of English theological fury, but might protect ourselves in the armour of virtuous reparation.

In some places an ancient "Priest's House" recalls the years when the parish priest dwelt near
his church in lonely poverty. But in most villages
and small towns the vicarage or rectory of the Established Church has developed into a dwelling-
place of happy stability, a home of ancient peace,
surrounded by a beautiful flower-garden, a useful
vegetable-garden, a paddock for the horse of a
humble vehicle, and, in later times, a tennis-court
for the clergyman's athletic sons, charming daughters, and the comfortable clergyman himself.[1] There
he lives, taking the services in his church, and keeping it clean and in good repair so far as his knowledge and funds allow, visiting the sick, consoling

---

[1] The standard mortality (basis 100) is for Anglican clergy 56, for coal-
miners 101, for seamen 177, for cutlery grinders 330.

the dying, giving good advice, and consulting with
his amiable wife upon the judicious relief of distress.
It is his duty to influence his curates, to restrain
their perturbing zeal, and to preach at least once a
week to his flock. He has been moderately educated
at Oxford or Cambridge, and the Church system is
still defended by many, as by Wordsworth, for supplying at least one educated gentleman in every village. The effect of his education upon the village
mind is illustrated by the villagers whom Tennyson knew in his younger days:

" An' I hallus coom'd to's chooch afore my Sally wur deäd,
　An' 'eärd 'um a bummin' awaäy loik a buzzard-clock ower
　　my 'eäd,
　An' I niver knaw'd whot a meän'd but I thowt a 'ad sum-
　　mat to saäy,
　An' I thowt a said whot a owt to a' said an' I coom'd
　　awaäy." [1]

Since the beginning of the last century, the som-
nolent acquiescence of the Established Church has
been greatly disturbed by three powerful "move-
ments"—the Evangelical, developed from the
teaching of John Wesley, an Oxford student; the
High Church or Anglican, developed from the teaching of Newman and Pusey in Oxford; and the scien-
tific or Broad Church, developed from the critical
teaching of Oxford scholars in *Essays and Reviews,*
and the naturalist teaching of Charles Darwin, a
Cambridge man. Thus the very training grounds of

[1] *The Northern Farmer* (Old Style).

the youthful clergy became implicated in doctrines
of pervasive force, and, as might be expected from
the English nature, of violently opposite tendencies.

The Evangelical influence was for many years
powerful throughout the country. It effected much
for the working people at home and the slaves in
the Colonies. Outside Clapham, I think it was
strongest in the North and the Midlands. At all
events, it was almost omnipotent there when I was
young, being naturally allied with the local Non-
conformity in doctrine, though separated by a definite social line. In those days the whole of our
life was tinged or dyed with religion, almost every
hour being pervaded with a sense of the Divine.
Family prayers were said morning and evening,
and at each, starting at different points, we read
the whole of the Bible steadily through, chapter by
chapter, omitting only the genealogies and the passages which might make the servants laugh. Every
day many verses from the most beautiful chapters
were learnt by heart, and every Sunday the family
attended two or even three long services in church,
sitting through prodigious sermons which de-
nounced sin and threatened sinners with eternal
damnation, which few could escape, for we had all
confessed ourselves miserable sinners.

The literal and historic truth of every word in the
Authorized Version of the Bible was believed without the impiety of question, and if anyone by acci-
dent knocked a Bible off a table, a hush ensued as

though the heavens fell. No interests counted in comparison with religion. What did Sport matter when the flames of Hell could almost be felt licking our feet? What did Politics matter when the only object in life was to gain salvation? Why waste time over other literature when we had been granted the Book written by the hand of God Himself, infinitely beyond the rivalry of human authors? Why be led astray by the fantasies of Art when the spirit worshipped most devoutly in solitude, or in the plainest and ugliest tabernacle that a building contractor could stick together?

The wonder was that a religion so pervasive and terrific did not overwhelm us all in a gloom such as haunted the poet Cowper's gentle soul beyond the limits of sanity. Yet I knew many healthy children to whom, like myself, this Vale of Tears was not entirely a scene of woe, even though the shadow of the approaching Sunday was felt as early as Thursday. The depression was counterbalanced by the joy of Sunday night, inspired by the secret thought that a whole week must pass before the next sermon, and meantime there were all manner of jolly things to do. That form of religion — a genuine and spiritual form, founded on the fear of the Lord, which is the beginning, though not the end, of wisdom — still lingers in parts of England, especially in the North, but the general change since my boyhood has been incalculable.

Outwardly, the most evident change in the

Established Church has been due to the influence of the High Church or Anglo-Catholic party, which, as a result of insistence upon different doctrines never so fully appreciated by the Evangelicals, has succeeded in restoring to the Church something of the pervasive beauty and æsthetic charm of the older Catholic ritual and symbolism. The restoration of the ancient buildings, the cultivation of choir music, unalloyed by congregational efforts to keep up with the organ, the introduction of sacerdotal vestments and altar-cloths, of flowers, shining brass utensils on the altar, images, pictures of the Stations, crucifixes, and incense as a symbol of adoration rather than a preventive of infection — all these attractive adjuncts to the Services in accordance with the Book of Common Prayer have accomplished much towards beautifying the churches and uplifting the spirit of their members.

It is another question how far the inward and spiritual doctrines believed to be symbolized by these æsthetic improvements have been accepted or realized by the English people. The distrust of the Roman Church is still deep. The Church Service no longer asks us to pray to be delivered from " the Bishop of Rome and all his detestable enormities," but the English hostility to all foreign authority, whether spiritual or political, subsists below the tolerant surface, and the Anglo-Catholics are sometimes condemned for making vain advances to Rome, as though an affectionate woman were re-

peatedly wooing an obstinately high-principled gentleman, who rejects any alliance on the terms she
proposes.

The underlying Protestantism of the English, especially regarding the doctrinal mystery of Tran-
substantiation, is often revealed, as by the rejection
of the Revised Prayer Book in the House of Commons (1928), and by the widespread protest against
the celebration of "High Mass" upon a football
ground in June, 1930. Or, to take an earlier instance: in 1909 the Romanists proposed to carry the
Host in procession through the streets round their
great cathedral in Westminster. As leader-writer on
the *Daily News,* I supported the proposal in the
name of religious toleration, though at the last moment Mr. Asquith forbade the procession for fear of
riot. But for some days following, the editor's table
was heaped with letters of righteous indignation, denouncing that article, "obviously emanating from
a Popish pen," as one "Constant Reader" expressed it. "Scratch an Englishman and you find a
Protestant" is still a true saying.

Having been brought up in a circle where hatred
of the Pope of Rome was surpassed only by hatred
of the "Tractarians" (as the Anglo-Catholics were
then called), I must support this saying by higher
authority. Professor George Santayana, quoted by
Dean Inge of St. Paul's, writes:

> "The Englishman, living in and by his inner man,
> can never be really a Catholic. If he likes to call himself

so, it is a fad like a thousand others, to which his inner man, so seriously playful, is prone to lend itself. He may go over to Rome on a spiritual tour, just as he might abscond for a year and live in Japan with a Japanese wife; but if he becomes a Catholic at heart, he is no longer the man he was. Words cannot measure the chasm which must henceforth separate him from everything at home. For an Englishman, with freedom and reserve and experiment in his blood, to go over to Rome is an essential suicide; the inner man must succumb first. Such an Englishman might become a saint, but only by becoming a foreigner."

As comment, Dean Inge remarks:

"It would indeed be absurd to suppose that all English people have the qualities which observers have found in the race. In every large denomination there are natural Catholics and natural Protestants. But it is impossible to converse long with a Catholic without being conscious of an unsurmountable barrier; and if we consider what that barrier is, we find that we cannot confidently appeal to those instincts and moral traditions which are the common heritage of all English people. Santayana's words, though somewhat exaggerated, express a real truth."[1]

The English are an orderly people. The phrase "Law and Order" is hackneyed to absurdity among us. But by one of the perplexing contradictions in our nature, we strongly object to authority, especially in spiritual doctrines. There we are all for "Private Judgment," and that is where the "unsurmountable barrier" between us and the Roman

[1] *England*, by William Ralph Inge, Dean of St. Paul's, p. 68 (1926).

Church is built. I have felt a similar barrier standing between me and clergymen of the English
Church, however broad-minded they might profess
themselves; and if two or three of the clergy are
gathered together, a separating wall rises round
them at once.

At the same time, in minds " naturally Catholic," the longing for the comfort of authority leads
to the Roman Church, and souls bewildered or
overburdened with spiritual doubts take refuge
there, finding relief in an authority above dispute.
" Securus judicat orbis terrarum." Who could question the judgment of a Church actually Catholic
or Universal?

Another disturbing force to assail the comfortable lethargy of the English Church was the sudden
development of morphology, geology, and literary
criticism in the middle of last century. After the
diffusion of the unsuspected truths revealed by
those sciences, it became impossible to maintain
many ecclesiastical dogmas hitherto laid down as
" fundamental." In regard to the literal and historic truth of the Hebrew writings loosely collected
as " The Bible," that was impossible, and the familiar Biblical stories became easy butts for the
half-educated wits who boasted themselves " Athe-
ists " because they no longer relied on the Garden
of Eden as historic, or because they had geological
qualms about the Flood. The section of the clergy
roughly called " Broad Church " boldly accepted

the revelations of natural and critical sciences, speedily discovering that the supposed "fundamentals" were of small spiritual value, or were capable of serviceable interpretation. For some years this attitude aroused much opposition. Every curate laboured to reconcile science with religion, and many abandoned Christianity through dubitations as to the Fiery Furnace. But, with her boasted "elasticity," the Church of England quietly assimilated the Broad Church clergy, the sceptics, Evolution, Geology, the Infinite Universe, and all. Earnest men and women, still calling themselves Christians, make no secret of unbelief for which our fathers would have willingly burnt them alive, and tending the same fold we may find a Bishop denouncing as barbarian magic a doctrine which other shepherds worship as the centre of all religious faith. Of the monastic vows, Obedience is not scrupulously observed, but the vow of Poverty is now more strictly imposed, and the temptations of worldliness are diminished by our national impoverishment.

To laymen it may seem that no definite Orthodoxy can prevail inside a Church where the shepherds are not unanimous, and the sheep so violently disagree that they might break through the wattles of the pen, were they not bound together by the Establishment. And yet many laymen, even though outside the fold, would regret a collapse which would entail much confusion, and a wide breach with tradition. The younger clergy are often found labouring at social improvements among the poorest of the workers, and the people think the better of the Church because they consider the effort well-intentioned, however vain, and however much disapproved even by the wisest of the clerical leaders.[1]

Even in villages where the rivalry between Church and Dissent follows the line of social caste and is therefore most embittered, the Dissenters often go to the church for christenings, marriages, and funerals on account of village tradition, or "to show a decent respect." And one can hardly exaggerate the value of the Church in maintaining from one vanishing generation to another the sense of beauty already mentioned — the beauty of the historic buildings themselves, of the music and the language, of the clerical dresses, and of the church bells heard from far off:

> "In summertime on Bredon
>   The bells they sound so clear;
> Round both the shires they ring them
>   In steeples far and near,
>   A happy sound to hear."[2]

The distrust of authority and the confidence in private judgment have naturally produced a larger number of religious sects in England than in any

---

[1] "I hold it a great mistake for a clergyman in a large town to engage in non-spiritual work, however desirable that work may be in itself."—Canon Peter Green of Manchester in *The Times, Church and Empire Number*, June 25, 1930, p. 23.

[2] *A Shropshire Lad; Bredon Hill.*

other country, except the United States, where the
sects are perhaps more numerous, and certainly
more peculiar. From before the Reformation onward without a break down to the formation of the
Salvation Army, nearly every sect has enjoyed the
privilege of persecution at the hands of the Roman
or the Anglican Church, and for the English people
persecution has more attraction than conviction.
Consequently, the Free, Nonconformist, or Dis-
senting bodies, if combined, would embrace the
great majority of the populace, especially in the
Northern counties. Except for the abhorrence of
" Popish ways," the division of the Nonconformists
from the Established Church is now almost as much
social as doctrinal. Owing to the comparatively high
education of her clergy, and their frequent relationship to the squires, even by marriage, the Church
has come to be regarded as peculiarly the domain of
the gentry, and if a Nonconformist family advances
in prosperity it often transfers its doctrinal convictions from the chapel to the parish church, or at-
tends the chapel in the morning, and the church at
night, when, indeed, the service is more beautiful,
and the hymns more familiar as being the poetry
of the English people.

The underlying religious passion of the race is revealed in these numerous sects, in the Salvation
Army (most at home in its native land, though
world-wide in influence), and in the hundreds or
thousands who gather near the Marble Arch in

Hyde Park and stand throughout the afternoon, especially on Saturdays and Sundays, listening intently to speakers and preachers who side by side uphold or denounce Christianity with equal vehemence, and in like manner attack or defend the Roman form of faith. It is noticeable that the old-fashioned persiflage of the Bible stories, once applauded among people of advanced views, is now seldom heard and never appreciated. People of advanced views have passed away into Rationalist or Ethical Societies, where the highest and most puzzling questions of metaphysics and morality are freely expounded or discussed, with interludes of music. How far such services represent or inculcate religion, I cannot determine. But they do represent a desire for spiritual truth. A different side of a similar desire is foreshadowed in the haunted regions of Spiritualism, Necromancy, and other ghostly investigations, much cultivated during the Great War under the anguishing anxiety for the safety of beloved men in peril, and since the War under the intense longing to renew some contact, however shadowy, with those whom the War prematurely snatched from sight.

Writers dispute as to the effect of the War upon the religious feeling of a people who lost nearly one million of their finest and youngest men out of their very midst. It seems impossible that the old unquestioning belief in a benign and omnipotent Divinity, or the belief in a special Providence that numbers

the hairs of every head should remain undimin-
ished. Among wealthy and aristocratic circles, in-
dustriously occupied in the contrivance of pleasures,
religion probably plays no great part now. And the
same may be said of the cultured circles industri-
ously occupied in contriving art and criticism. But
the War could not reduce the religious feeling in
either circle, since neither felt a need of it before.
Among productive people, the working classes and
the men of action, the religious sense probably subsists silently in the English way, though the aspect
of religion as of all Nature has deepened and
widened, making the faith less simple. It has always
been hard to estimate the present or the future of
any religious form. Tacitus, wisest of Romans in his
day, dismissed Christianity in a scornful paragraph.
Browning represented his Cleon in the same period
as supposing the doctrine of St. Paul and Christ
could be held by no sane man. To think of Dryden's
poem again, religion has been like the Milk-
white Hind, " Doomed to death, though fated not
to die."

Indeed, the philosopher, Professor Rudolf
Eucken, goes so far as to say: " We not only can
be, but must be Christians; only, however, if we
recognize that Christianity is a progressive development still in the making." [1]

We must also recognize that natural Science and
Art can inspire a genuine religious sense, as is evi-

---

[1] Quoted by Dean Inge in *Points of View*, p. 44 (1930).

dent when a man of science, Mr. J. B. S. Haldane, Reader in Biochemistry at Cambridge, writes:

> "If I thought that the aims of science and art were merely material I should belong to some church. But I believe that the scientist is trying to express absolute truth and the artist absolute beauty, so that I find in science and art, and in an attempt to lead a good life, all the religion that I want." [1]

With that Confession of Faith one may compare the wise saying of Goethe: "The man who has science or art has also religion. The man who has neither science nor art, should have religion."

All Continental races charge the English with religious hypocrisy. It has become a useful and well-worn tag among their journalists, especially in Paris. Hypocrisy has been defined as the tribute that vice pays to virtue, and, to listen to our foreign satirists, one might suppose the English pay to virtue not a tribute but reparations in mass. The charge has arisen from a misunderstanding of the English nature, so varied in thought and so contradictory in conduct. Our beliefs and rules are so numerous and so diverse that one section of the people may be thinking and acting in flat opposition to another, and all to each. What is even more puzzling, similar contradictions may co-exist in the same man. So the absence of logical principle produces the appearance of hyprocrisy, though the supposed hypocrite is not acting a sanctimonious part,

[1] *Ibid.*, p. 75.

but simply following one natural line of his character in contradiction to another. On the other hand, we must admit, perhaps with pride, that our creative genius has produced a typical hypocrite in Pecksniff, just as the French genius has produced one in Tartuffe, though no one charges the French with hypocrisy.

IV. ART

> " He dipped his brush and tried to fix a line,
>   And then came peace, and gentle beauty came,
>   Turning his spirit's water into wine,
>   Lightening his darkness with a touch of flame.
>   O, joy of trying for beauty, ever the same,
>   You never fail, your comforts never end;
>   O, balm of this world's way; O, perfect friend!"
>
> John Masefield's *Dauber*, III.

Many foreigners repeat the mistake of describing the English as " practical," " hard-headed," " material," or " a nation of shopkeepers," as though we were indifferent to art and incapable of beauty. We have brought the reproach upon ourselves by our inherent modesty in regard to the arts, and a feeling that there is something effeminate and unreal about them. If a young man announces that he intends to be a painter or a poet, we look upon him with suspicion and regret, as likely to be futile, disappointed, and poor. We should much rather hear him say he meant to pursue medicine or even theology, or, best of all, that he would read and

" eat his dinners " (strange qualification!) for the bar. That would set him on a level with all other young men who do not know what to do. But Art! That is no occupation for a virile Englishman! "Back to your gallipots, boy!" cried the critic to Keats.

Yet the whole race has from the earliest times overflowed with imagination and romance. What a wealth of poetic sweetness and gaiety lies in the names of our common flowers — Love-in-a-mist, Love-lies-bleeding, Love-in-idleness, Forget-me-not, Heartsease, Honeysuckle, Lady's Smock, Lady's Slipper, Shepherd's Purse, Ragged Robin, Bridget-in-her-Bravery, Traveller's Joy, Solomon's Seal, Lords and Ladies, Milkmaids, Meadow-sweet, and Blowsy Bess! What consoling jollity in the saying, " Grand weather for ducks! " or " It's raining cats and dogs! "

And just as these names and sayings grew out of the heart of a poetic and imaginative people, so the music and words of the folk-songs grew, and the music and figures of the folk-dances, whether " country," " morris," or " sword." Most of the songs and ballads, that sprang up spontaneously as the scarlet toadstools in the forests, told of love or the sea. Some of the love-songs, such as " Blow away the morning dew " and " William Taylor," are touched with mockery, but as a rule they are simple and straightforward expressions of the common passion, usually suggesting, without any preface or explanation, some scene of meeting among the meadows or by the riverside, as in " Searching for Lambs " or " Mowing the Barley," or the beautiful version of "Waly, Waly" beginning "The Water is wide, I cannot get o'er." Sometimes a tale of sorrow is hidden in the song, as in " The Sprig of Thyme " and " The Trees they do grow high," both songs of great beauty. More seldom they tell of the universal fate, as in " Death and the Lady " which, like so many, begins with the simple scene, " As I walked out one day, one day." And some of the ballads are tragic, as " Lord Rendal " and the version of "Edward, Edward," beginning "How comes that blood on your shirt-sleeve? " But we hear only gaiety and spring and freedom in "The Cuckoo she's a pretty bird" and "The Wraggle-Taggle Gipsies, O."

Then, as to the sea, perhaps sea-songs appear specially numerous because Cecil Sharp, the finest collector of English songs and dances, gathered so many memories of them on the sea-coast of Somerset. Some, such as " My Bonny Lighter Boy " and " The Bold Fisherman," are simple love-songs of a maid and a sea-faring lover. But many are daring ballads that seem to belong to the dashing eighteenth century of pressgangs, rollicking sailors with their wenches in every port, and glorious victories over pirates and the French. Such are " The Coasts of High Barbary," " The Golden Vanity," the bull-dog ballad of "Admiral Benbow," and the joyful home-sailing song of "Spanish Ladies," with its irresistible chorus:

"We'll rant and we'll roar like true British sailors,
  We'll rant and we'll roar all on the salt seas,
  Until we strike soundings in the channel of old England,
  From Ushant to Scilly is thirty-five leagues."

There are, besides, the numerous old Shanties or Chanteys, like "Shanandoah" and "Won't you go my Way?" which helped the weighing of the anchor, or hauling the ropes; and we must not forget the riddle songs, as "I gave my love a cherry without a stone," or "Say, can you make me a cambric shirt?" and the "Accumulative Songs," as "One man shall mow my Meadow" and "The Tree in the Wood." For in those riddling songs and adding-up songs we come near that peculiar love of nonsense so characteristic of the English genius. It springs only from genius as seen in the Shakespearian Fools, Lear's *Book of Nonsense,* Lewis Carroll's *Alice in Wonderland,* and the other two inspired works of that rather prim and starchy don, who vainly tried to infuse elementary mathematics into Christ Church undergraduates.

It is hard in mere words to give any conception of the skill and beauty expressed in the various forms of folk-dance, also preserved to us by the persistent devotion of Cecil Sharp. So we have the English Sword Dances (no relations to the Scottish), to be traced back into the sacrificial and bloody rites

solemnly practised among our prehistoric ancestors;
the energetic Morris Dances, of unknown origin,
but perhaps connected with a dark-skinned people,
like Moors, or more likely with the faces smeared
for impersonality; and the freer and more beautiful Country Dances, that seem to have grown up
like daisies on the village greens, apparently to fit
the songs familiar at the time. It is hard to choose
the best instances among so many good, but anyone would name — "Step Stately," "Old Noll's
Jig," "Green Sleeves," "Newcastle," and "Old
Mole."

The songs, music, and dances, which evidently
abounded in mediæval and Elizabethan England,
were scattered by the Puritan incursion of ascetic
religion, but were transfigured into other forms as
we see in Purcell, in the great popularity of Handel,
and in the satiric operas of Gilbert and Sullivan,
who combined to express the melody, the humour,
and the love of nonsense inherent in our race.
Further evidence of our feeling for rollicking music
may be heard in any church or chapel where the
congregations shout with gusto the martial hymns,
"Onward Christian Soldiers," or "The Son of God
goes forth to War," and songs of hopeful assurance
such as "Shall we gather at the River," and "O
Paradise, O Paradise, who doth not crave for rest,"
though the patriotic and vigorous English people
picture the river as a Thames or a Severn, and the
last thing they crave for is rest in death. A kindred

musical zeal is shown by the Yorkshire Choral Societies and the crowds who stand for hours closely
packed together in the Queen's Hall of London, listening to Bach.

English architecture, however much influenced
by Norman and French, always had a peculiar
beauty of its own, chiefly the beauty of simplicity,
and like all true art, it grew from style to style by
a natural and unconscious development in tradition. The beauty of our sculpture, fresco, carving,
manuscript, and metal work has lately been revealed in the collection of English Mediæval Art
in the Victoria and Albert Museum (1930), where
England could be recognized as once a workshop
and still a treasure-house of art, though American
wealth has carried much away. But that exhibition
brought no surprise to those who year by year had
quietly consorted with our cathedrals and the
churches of old towns and villages. It is obvious
that, with the expansion of knowledge and the decay of primitive faith, our Catholic art began to
decay, but art itself took new forms in the Elizabethan and Queen Anne mansions, in public buildings, in the classic churches of Wren, and in Georgian halls and gardens. The self-conscious attempts
to keep pace with the last century's Anglican movement by a Gothic revival in architecture may appear
rather amusing than admirable, but, except for the
Victorian gap, the building art has never died among
us and is now developing to match the development

of life. The bungalow, it is true, which is the latest and most popular development, suggests connubial bliss rather than beauty.

Painting in England has followed much the same course as our architecture, moving from period to period on a general line of tradition. In both arts, if you see a specimen of one or other, you can almost certainly tell its date within ten years, and that shows how lively and adventurous the art has been. Most of the arts, but especially painting, seem to move, advance or retrogress by a succession of reactions — reaction from religious subjects to classical subjects; from classical to domestic subjects; from domestic to mystical subjects; from mystical subjects to dogs and deer; from animals to pretty representations and edifying tales; from prettiness to power, and from edifying tales to representations of nothing. All these forms have been followed and welcomed in their turn, though the dogs, darlings, and domestic tales have always been most beloved, because the whole English people love dogs, darlings, and happy endings. And we must not forget the continuous popularity of the "Tally-ho pictures" — scenes of fox-hunting, racing, and old coaching days. They are to be found in every country inn, in country houses, and in one old and prosperous shop in Piccadilly. A good portrait of a favourite horse is still rewarded as highly as a good portrait of a favourite woman.

But among all these shifting scenes, styles, and

and investigators in Natural Science, whose works have changed the speculation of the world, and who have none the less written comprehensibly. In the art of history we thought Gibbon had produced a monumental work until our historic science grew so extensively that a leading historian lately informed us Gibbon was " quite good for an amateur."

About once a year, apart from the dominant Irishman's works, some Englishman produces a good play for the theatre, such as *The Fanatics, Young Woodley*, and *Journey's End,* but till lately the huge shadow of Shakespeare has rather overwhelmed our stage, like a cathedral in a village of comfortable cottages. For the cinema, the English have produced the finest scenes of actual life among wild beasts and wild birds. But in imaginative film dramas we have hitherto been beaten by the Germans, Russians, and Hollywood. Not aiming so high as the Germans or the Russians, nor so low as the Americans, our designers of plots seldom succeed in reaching either the intelligent or the vulgar audiences, and for the "talkies " the gentler English voice appears not to carry so well as the American penetrating sounds. But we must not forget that Charlie Chaplin, the universal comedian of the films, both as author and actor, welcomed in every country of the world, was, like Dickens, an Englishman born and bred.

Dress is a form of art, and in the Middle Ages the dress of the gentry was noble and distinctive, as were their others arts. A grotesque period followed, but men's dress retained a certain comeliness till the beginning of last century, when it degenerated into a hideous uniformity that changes subtly, but seldom for the better. This is all the more deplorable because the English gentleman, as we saw in a preceding chapter, sets the fashion which Continental and American nations pant after in vain. In spite of all the protests of common sense, nearly all of us still conceal the beauty of our legs in long cloth cylinders; we still throttle our necks in starchy collars, and our bodies in starchy shirts; and on solemn occasions, such as Court functions, marriages, funerals, and cricket matches we still dishonour our heads with the ugliest covering ever invented outside the Solomon Islands or the habit of Orthodox priests, who wear their top hats upside down.

But, perhaps owing to their rapid emancipation in politics, athletics, and companionship with men, English women have advanced far from the upholstery of dress fashionable in the last century, and at the passing moment they easily surpass men in beauty and good-sense of costume. They leave their throats finely open to sun and air, allowing the blood to flow freely up to the brain. So far as one can tell, there is not an inch of solid starch about them. They wear small and sensible hats, over which they and we can see the stage without obstacle. And do they conceal the beauty of their legs? They do not. (Written at 12.30 p.m., July 3, 1930; forecast, " unsettled.")

CHAPTER X

THE ENGLISH BASE

AMONG A race of so many million men and women, each differing in body and soul from the next, it is hard to fix upon any characteristic that can be called general. As a whole, the English have a physical courage that always amazes me, and I have seen it unconsciously displayed on many terrible occasions in peace and war. They have a moral courage, which I suppose is the basis of all virtues. They have a power of endurance, which Napoleon placed higher than courage among the virtues of the soldier, and which has been repeatedly shown in exploration as on campaigns. They have more self-control in speech and action than I have found among southern races, and they are at least as honest as other people. Without rising to Mr. Podsnap's height of patriotic eulogy, one may call these qualities admirable.

But as their most distinctive possessions I should choose irony and humour. These are almost universal among the working people, and it is among the working people that we must look for typical qualities, since they compose the majority of the English.

The upper class have irony and humour too, though not in such copious abundance. As I have noticed, the middle classes are often deficient in the sense of both, and I can see no reason for the want, unless it is a freezing fear of vulgarity and loss of caste, which neither the upper nor working classes feel. The Shakespearian Fools, especially the Fool in *King Lear*, and the common soldiers in the historical plays abound in English irony. And speaking of soldiers, one remembers them in the Great War — all the millions from the typical working classes. How ironical they were! In the front trenches the filthiest and most dangerous dug-outs were usually labelled " Windsor Castle," " Buckingham Palace," " The Carlton," " The Ritz," " Health Resort," " The Sanatorium," or " The Abode of Love." In the South African War we sang, " Oh, why did I leave my little back room in Bermondsey? " and " I study in economy and live like a lord." And no one who lived through the Great War can forget the soldiers' songs. Early in the war we had the one beginning " Send out the Army and the Navy," and ending the chorus with " Send out my mother, my sister, and my brother, but for Gord's sake don't send me! " Later on there was a very popular song capable of infinite extension and variety, beginning " Have you seen the sergeant " (or the general, or whom you will) ; " I know where he is, I know where he is, I know where he is. Have you seen the sergeant? I know where he is, Laying on the canteen floor " (or any other situation to taste). Another not so familiar, formed on the model of " The House that Jack Built " ran in the culminating verse:

"Now Old King Cole was a merry old soul, and a merry old soul was he;
He called for a pipe and he called for a bowl, and he called for his generals three;
Now every general had a fine voice, and a very fine voice had he,
  'The Army's going to the dogs,' said the generals;
  'What's the next word of command?' said the colonels;
  'Blankety-blankety-blank!' said the majors;
  'May I go on leave for a month?' said the captains;
  'We do all the work!' said the subalterns;
  'Move to the right in fours!' said the sergeants;
  'Left-right-left-right-left!' said the corporals;
  'Beer! Beer! Beer!' said the privates;
  Jolly fine chaps are we!
There's none so rare as can compare
With the boys of the King's Armee! "

I believe that song sprang from the academic shades of Oxford and originally ended " With the O.U.O. T.C."

But more characteristic in its pathetic irony was the well-known dirge beginning " I want to go home, I want to go home," and ending, " Oh my, I don't want to die, I want to go home, I want to go home! " But if an enemy, hearing that chorus wailed across the top, had attacked confident of a victory over " defeatists," he would have made a great mistake.

The true Cockney can hardly speak or think without irony. When someone has been terribly hurt, the Cockney will observe, " He didn't 'alf 'oller! " When someone had been killed on the Tube, the Cockney accurately reported, "Traffic was delayed 14 minutes." Understatement is a favourite form, as in the common phrases " Not 'alf! " and " I don't think! " (which is not so new as it sounds, for Sam Weller uses it). On the other hand there is magnificence in "Lansbury's Lido " as a title for the bathing place on the Serpentine, and Cockney splendour shines in a conversation heard last June in a little grocer's shop off Gray's Inn Road:

> "And where," asked the genial grocer of the unemployed labourer's wife, whom he was "obliging," as he often does with her weekly stores on account: "Where are you takin' your summer holiday this year? Riviera again? " "Well," was the ready answer, "I did think of takin' a run down there in my Rolls-Royce to 'ave a look at the bathin' costumes." "To be sure, yes," said the grocer, while he packed bacon and tea and sugar and pink salmon and "condensed" into her bag, as politely as though he were going to be paid on the spot: "I hear they're worth inspection — what there is of 'em, that is. Begin here, and end there, so I'm told."

English irony reached its literary height in Dean Swift's *Voyage to Laputa,* but, though we find it in many of our finest characters, such as Falstaff and Mrs. Gamp, and the creations of Jane Austen and Thomas Hardy, it does not pervade our literature

so widely as our daily life. We may connect with it the peculiar English habit of cutting words and sentences short, as though to avoid rhetoric. "Pram," "bus," "doc," and "bike" are obvious examples, and when a girl tells me she has just been "permed," meaning she has lately had permanent undulations applied to her hair, I recognize her race. "Peach-perch" is a pleasing name for the girl's pillion behind a motor-cycle, and it commends a cake to be told it "eats short." I like to recall the brevity of my nursemaid, who, when I was fractious about my food, used to say, "If you don't want it now, you must eat it against you do." I like our summary use of "it," as when one of our poets, T. E. Brown, sings "Oh, blackbird, how you do go it!" Or when in a cricket match the posters proclaimed "Peebles did it!" Or when at a national crisis we say, "We mean to see it through." And I like the Cockney's quick repartee when the guard, anxious that no one should go wrong, cried, "All right, Leatherhead?" "Quite, thank you, Kipper-face!" replied the passenger.

Irony appears to spring from our deeply rooted qualities of reserve and self-control. I have mentioned instances in an earlier chapter, but two more may be given to illustrate the horror of display or gestures in our highest and our lower classes. On Mr. Arthur Balfour's first mission to America during the Great War, with Sir Tom Bridges as military member, it happened that the French mission

led by Maréchal Joffre and M. Viviani were there at
the same time, and Sir Ian Malcolm narrates what
happened:

> "On one occasion M. Viviani was speaking to a great
> meeting in Chicago, and his speech roused old Maréchal
> Joffre to such a pitch of emotion that, at its conclusion,
> the man of war embraced the man of words on both
> cheeks. I was reading an account of this demonstration
> to A. J. B. as we drove down to the Senate, where he
> was to give an address. He listened, and then said
> solemnly: 'Ian, whatever I say this morning or whatever
> I do, I count on you to prevent Tom Bridges from kissing
> me.'" [1]

The other instance is happily familiar, but for
English tradition and proud self-control it cannot
be beaten. An English private was brought as pris-
oner before a high Chinese dignitary, and com-
manded to kowtow on penalty of execution. "We
don't do that sort of thing in the Buffs," he answered,
and died.

On the other hand, to show how tender may be
the feelings protected by the stern husk of our self-
control, I may recall an epitaph I discovered under
the pavement matting in the great church of Dorchester, where the Thame joins the Isis:

> "Reader!
> If thou hast a heart fam'd for tenderness and pity
>   Contemplate this spot
> In which are deposited the Remains of a Young Lady

[1] *Lord Balfour: a Memory*, by Sir Ian Malcolm. (Quoted in *The Times*
of June 21, 1930.)

Whose artless Beauty, Innocence of Mind, and gentle
    Manners
    Once obtained for her the Love and Esteem of all who
        knew her.
        But when nerves were too delicately spun to bear the
        rude shakes and jostlings which we meet with in this
        transitory World, Nature gave way; She sunk and died,
A Martyr to excessive Sensibility.
  Mrs. Sarah Fletcher, wife of Captain Fletcher, departed
this life at the village of Clifton on June 7, 1799, in the 29th
year of her age.
    May her soul meet that peace in Heaven which this
        Earth denied her."

What were those rude shakes and jostlings, I wonder? And did the Captain compose the epitaph?

But in our official and business letters and in our
public speeches we retain habits of circumlocution
and insincere politeness. " I venture to suggest,"
" With all respect," " If I may say so," " The Right
Honourable Gentleman will forgive me if I remind him," " Of course I may be wrong," " Without fear of contradiction," and " I remain your
Lordship's humble and obedient servant " — how
pompous, how painful in futility such traditions
from the eighteenth century have become!

To speak of English humour would be to review
and analyse the whole of English nature, of which
humour is the soul or essence. It is the air we
breathe, the atmosphere from which we dare not escape, for without it we should stiffen into pedants
and doctrinaires, fit only for the mummy-cloths. As

easy to define life as English humour, and those who do not live in it can never learn. It has little to do with laughter, and little with gaiety. It hardly smiles, and some have said it weeps more often. But they exaggerate, for it has too much self-control and modesty to weep, or to use any outward gesture. There is no hatred in it, and no contempt or satire, but when we have said it implies affection, irony, quiet fun, and perhaps a touch of pity, we are not much nearer the reality.

Even the finest literary examples cannot explain a quality of which we see the living incarnations around us in every street and house. We take Falstaff as the highest embodiment of humour, but we may find a better round the corner or in our own room. And the example of Falstaff suggests another question. He knew that he was humorous himself and the cause of humour in others. Dr. Johnson knew that too. But did Uncle Toby? He was a very type of English humour, and his brother, Mr. Shandy, recognized it, but Uncle Toby would not have thought himself humorous, nor would Mr. Shandy. Nor would Mrs. Gamp, or Susan Nipper, or Mrs. Nickleby, or Justice Shallow. I am not sure about Nick Bottom, Dick Swiveller, or the elder Mr. Weller, but I doubt if Mr. Micawber was conscious how humorous a figure he was, and certainly Mrs. Micawber had no notion of it. So that it may need two to realize humour, just as it is said to need two to realize a Scotsman's joke, one being English.

We could not call Milton or Shelley or Tennyson humorists, but most of our permanent writers, including even our prophets like Ruskin and Carlyle, are kept alive by their humour, and humour so inspires a letter from Lamb as to outlive a philosophy. But even examples cannot define a habit of mind so pervasive — an atmosphere in which the English have their being.[1]

During the last century the English caricaturists have advanced in humour, if humour implies kindliness. We should not now expect of them, or even tolerate, the cruelty and grotesque exaggeration of Rowlandson, Gillray, or the early Cruikshank, who, unfortunately, spread so false an impression of Dickens by his pitiful illustrations. Since then the advance in real humour has been marked by Leech, Keene, Du Maurier, Tenniel, F. C. Gould, up to "Max," the subtlest of artist-caricaturists, and to "Low," in hopes of finding one of whose passing shots we daily gamble a penny on an evening paper. And with the finest caricaturists one may class the English clowns, welcomed throughout Europe, and rising to the height in Charlie Chaplin, sometimes clown, sometimes comedian, and often embodying the very soul of English humour that neither laughs nor weeps in outward show, but in spirit laughs and weeps together, like the fog and sunshine of a London day.

[1] *English Humour*, by J. B. Priestley (1929), is an admirable volume devoted to this theme.

A growth of self-control as another element of humour is proved by the reduced drunkenness since the beginning of this century. Compared with the year before the Great War this reduction is remarkable, for the figures show 188,877 convictions for drunkenness in 1913 and only 55,642 in 1928 (England and Wales), in spite of a great increase in population.[1] Poverty and taxation may partly account for this difference, and no doubt the pleasures of the cinema and motor-coaches have contributed, but the reduction is so extraordinary that it seems to show a change in the habits of the working people such as was seen among the upper classes early last century, and still persists in spite of cocktail parties. But habits, whether innocent or of excess, change slowly in a people so enthralled by tradition as the English are. Byron was not a model of our traditional ways, but he liked to have hot-cross-buns on Good Friday, and roast goose on Michaelmas Day.[2]

As for the fellow-feeling and sympathy which also go to the making of humour, everyone who has lived with our soldiers knows how common and unostentatious they are. Unhappily, there is no such comradeship in the world as in war, and the sooner the world discovers some substitute for war the better, if it will produce the fellowship of soldiers. But

[1] See the Licensing Statistics issued by the Home Office, September 20, 1929.

[2] *Byron*, by André Maurois, Vol. II, page 208.

in ordinary life the English common people are kindly and free from rancour. They remind me of the Romans who always put their word for hating (*odisse*) in the perfect tense; I cannot tell why, unless to suggest that hatred should always be a thing of the past. Similarly after the Great War the main body of the English people got over their hatred quickly, and retained neither animosity nor thoughts of vengeance. In Cologne just after the Armistice I saw an English soldier go up to a German child and say: " Come 'ere, you square-headed little bastard of a bloody 'Un! I'm goin' to slit your bloody throat!" Whereupon the child, not understanding our language, held out its hand in confident expectation of what was to follow, and the bit of chocolate followed. "There's our sentimental Tommy!" I thought. It is true that this sort of kindliness may slop over into the sickening sentimentality of our most popular pictures, plays, and books; but kindly fair-play in itself is not necessarily a bad quality. One recalls the answer of Tom Cribb, the invincible prize-fighter, when he was assaulted by someone in a crowd: " I can't hit you," he said, " I'm Tom Cribb!"

And to sum up: there are a few lines in John Masefield's description of the huntsman, Robin Dawe, that express much of the English character:

> "His face was of the country mould
> Such as the mason sometimes cutted
> On English moulding-ends which jutted

Out of the church walls centuries since.
And as you never know the quince,
How good he is until you try,
So in Dawe's face, what met the eye
Was only part; what lay behind
Was English character and mind,
Great kindness, delicate sweet feeling
(Most shy, most clever in concealing
Its depth) for beauty of all sorts,
Great manliness and love of sports,
A grave, wise thoughtfulness and truth,
A merry fun outlasting youth,
A courage terrible to see,
And mercy for his enemy." [1]

And without exposing myself to the embarrassing charge of patriotism — embarrassing because it sounds inane to make defence against it — I may confess that often upon returning to England after long wanderings in other lands I have known the feelings finely expressed by Miss Amy Johnson in her wireless speech at Brisbane:

"When I saw the shores of Australia I shouted for joy; and the moment I landed I was greeted by my own people, who spoke my own language, with ideas the same as my own, and who met me with love and friendship in their hearts." [2]

"With ideas the same as my own." That is the secret of nationality and of English patriotism. For

[1] *Reynard the Fox*, p. 47 (1st edition).
[2] Quoted by Mr. Stanley Baldwin in a speech to the Fourth Imperial Press Conference, June 16, 1930.

it is only among English people that the English can understand or be understood.

In writing of my own countrymen I may well be charged with that amount of patriotism. In thinking of England I should much rather shout for joy like Miss Amy Johnson than give way to what Wordsworth called " unfilial fears." I should prefer to leave to gloomy prophets and mournful prognosticators the easy task of making us tremble with fears, regrets and dubitations. But even Wordsworth, in his famous sonnet of 1802, went on to admit that at times such fears would still recur because he felt for his country as a Lover or a Child. The daily life of every lover and every child is haunted by fears that spring from overwhelming affection and from a passionate desire for the loved one's highest good. And so for his country the patriot may fear lest she should sacrifice her noble traditions for avaricious gain, and degrade her reputation for courage by outbursts of cruel ferocity, and bedim her splendid vision of adventurous enterprise by stooping to the muckrake of comfortable satisfactions.

INDEX

INDEX

A
NOTE
ON THE
TYPE IN
WHICH THIS
BOOK IS SET

*This book has been
set in a modern ad-
aptation of a type de-
signed by William
Caslon, the first (1692–
1766), who, it is generally
conceded, brought the old-style
letter to its highest perfection.
An artistic, easily-read type,
Caslon has had two centuries of
ever-increasing popularity in our own
country—it is of interest to note that
the first copies of the Declaration of Independence and the first paper currency
distributed to the citizens of the new-born
nation were printed in this type face.*

SET UP, ELECTROTYPED, PRINTED, AND
BOUND BY THE PLIMPTON PRESS, NORWOOD, MASS.
PAPER MADE BY S. D. WARREN CO., BOSTON